God's Word to Man
A Translation, not a Version

WHY THE KING JAMES BIBLE IS THE ACCURATE ENGLISH BIBLE

By Stephen R. Gentry

Address All Inquiries To:
THE OLD PATHS PUBLICATIONS, INC.
142 Gold Flume Way
Cleveland, Georgia, U.S.A.

Web: www.theoldpathspublications.com
E-mail: TOP@theoldpathspublications.com

PREFACE

Since 1611, over 350 versions of the Bible have been printed in English. In this book, I will endeavor to explain that the King James Bible is not simply another version of the Bible but an actual translation from the original manuscripts into English. The original manuscripts of the Bible were written in Hebrew (the Old Testament) and Greek (the New Testament). The King James translation completely and accurately translates the Word of God into English.

The King James Bible is the Authorized Version of the English Bible. It acquired this name because it was authorized by King James to be the official English Bible, and it was to be used in all the Churches of England. The title page of the original 1611 King James Bible reads as follows:

The Holy Bible

Containing the Old Testament and the New

Newly Translated out of the Original

tongues and with former Translations

diligently compared and reviewed by his

Majesties special Commandment.

Since it is a translation and not a version, God's word is empowered. 2 Tim. 3:16-17, *"All scripture is given by inspiration of God, and is profitable for doctrine, for reproof, for correction, for instruction in righteousness: That the man of God may be perfect, throughly furnished unto all good works."* The original Scriptures were inspired, and God anoints every correctly translated verse from the original. The King James Bible is just as anointed today as it was when it was translated into English.

It might be well to note that any time God communes with man, not one of his words is wasted. Although we often use filler words to fill up space, with God, every word is sacred and purposeful. Therefore, it is of the utmost importance to have a word-for-word translation of the Bible. (In contrast to a translation, a version of the Bible will try to communicate an idea or principle of scripture rather than a direct translation. But when anyone gives their version of scripture, it is limited to their interpretation and can be intentionally or unintentionally misrepresented.) However, the King James Bible gives you an exact word-for-word translation. That allows the reader to interpret the Word of God for themselves.

Alexander McClure, in the introductory narrative of his book, *The Translators Revived*, made this statement about the King James Bible, "this blessed book is so far complete and exact, that the unlearned reader, being of ordinary intelligence, may enjoy the delightful assurance, that if he studies it in faith and prayer, and give himself up to its teachings, he shall not be confounded or misled as to any matter essential to his salvation and his spiritual good." *1

Since the King James Bible is a word-for-word translation, you do not need to be a Hebrew or Greek scholar to understand the Scriptures. You can rest assured that the translators were thorough and their motives pure while accomplishing this monumental task of Bible translation. Still, as an aid to studying the Bible, I would suggest a Webster's Dictionary and a Strong Exhaustive Concordance. With these resources, you can read and understand God's word as was intended.

This work is a thorough yet simplistic explanation of the preservation of God's Word. It deals with the journey of God's Word from its conception to its translation into English by order of King James VI of Scotland & I of England. For the teacher, I pray that it is a guide; for the student, I pray that it is informative; for the theologian, I pray it is correct; for the critic, I pray it is convincing.

*1 Alexander Wilson McClure, The Translators Revived, 1853, pg. 64-65

FOREWORD

In my thirty years of ministry, the question of why I prefer the King James Bible has come up many times. With so many versions available, it is understandable how a new student of God's word might be perplexed. What sets this one bible apart from other bibles? *God's Word to Man - A Translation, not a Version*, is a look into the accuracy of the King James Bible.

I have known Pastor Stephen Gentry for many years. First as a friend and now as my pastor. The history and translation of the King James Bible have been a passion of Pastor Gentry for many years. He has developed lessons and sermons on this topic and shared them with multiple groups and congregations. That divinely inspired passion has culminated in *God's Word to Man - A Translation, not a Version*. In these pages, Pastor Gentry carefully takes us along the path from God speaking to our English translation of that Holy Word. With an insightful look into the translators, their commission, and their methods of translating, he lays out why the King James Bible is the accurate English Bible.

Whether you are just curious about the topic or a serious student of God's word, *God's Word to Man - A Translation, not a Version* will be a powerful addition to your collection of books.

Joey Dean
January 2023

DEDICATION

This book is dedicated to my father:

He was an old-time Holiness preacher. I never heard him read or preach from any Bible except King James. He passionately believed in the inerrant Word of God.

Stephen R. Gentry
January 2023

Willie Ray Gentry (1935-1995)

TABLE OF CONTENTS

CHAPTER 1

GOD'S WORD TO MAN

Verbal Communication

Genesis 1:26,

And God said, Let us make man in our image, after our likeness: and let them have dominion over the fish of the sea, and over the fowl of the air, and over the cattle, and over all the earth, and over every creeping thing that creepeth upon the earth.

Creation, what a powerful thought. God spoke into existence the heaven, the earth, and all that was therein. There was not one flaw in all that he did. Genesis 1:31 says,

"And God saw every thing that he had made, and behold it was very good."

It is truly awe-inspiring when we realize that God, the creator of the earth and all it contains, took the dust of his creations and formed man. He made man in his image and His likeness because he would become a living soul when he would soon breathe into him. Man would be given the ability and intelligence to have dominion over every creature made by God, and most importantly, he would be able to communicate with God.

The first form of communication that Adam had with God was verbal. There is nothing more powerful than a face-to-face conversation. Gen. 2:15 states that God put man in the Garden of Eden to dress it and to keep it. Through communication, God told Adam that the garden would need pruning, watering, and tilling. These jobs were a pleasure until after sin defiled humanity, at which point, the ground became cursed with thorns and thistles, and by the sweat of the brow, man now eats his bread. God spoke to Adam and Eve in Gen. 1:28-30

> *28. And God blessed them, and God said unto them, Be fruitful, and multiply, and replenish the earth, and subdue it: and have dominion over the fish of the sea, and over the fowl of the air, and over every living thing that moveth upon the earth. 29. And God said, Behold, I have given you every herb bearing seed, which is upon the face of all the earth, and every tree, in the which is the fruit of a tree yielding seed; to you it shall be for meat. 30. And to every beast of the earth, and to every fowl of the air, and to every thing that creepeth upon the earth, wherein there is life, I have given every green herb for meat: and it was so.*

These scriptures reveal that God verbally communicated instructions to man. First, start a family, multiply, and replenish the earth. Secondly, to use the resources that the earth provided, subdue the earth. And lastly, to take dominion over the fish of the sea, the fowl of the air, and the beast of the field, to use these for work and food.

Gleaning from Gen. 3:8, The voice of the Lord could be heard walking in the garden in the cool of the day. This was not a strange thing or an unexpected happening but a time of considerable expectations. Sin would soon change communication forever.

One conversation is recorded in Gen. 2:16-17

And the Lord God commanded the man, saying, Of every tree of the garden thou mayest freely eat: 17 But of the tree of the knowledge of good and evil, thou shalt not eat of it: for in the day that thou eatest thereof thou shalt surely die.

People often think that God would only talk to Adam and Eve about the beauties of heaven and the mysteries of creation; however, these scriptures give us an insight into the seriousness of communicating with God.

First, the good news; *"of every tree of the garden thou mayest freely eat."* God has good things for those that serve him. Pr. 10:22, *"The blessing of the Lord, it maketh rich and he addeth no sorrow with it."* God purposely planted every tree that was pleasant to the sight and good for food in Eden. Not only did God plant every tree, but the Bible says a river went out from Eden to water the garden. Matthew Henry said, "Observe, that which God plants. He will take care to keep watered."

Not only was there a blessing promised, but commandments were also given, **"but of the tree of the knowledge of good and evil, thou shalt not eat of it."**

God spoke very directly, leaving no doubts about his intention. DO NOT EAT OF IT! Knowing that the eating of this tree was an offense to God was enough to drive Adam away from it. When his love for God was fervent, there was no problem keeping the commandment of the Lord.

Then there was the penalty, *"for in the day that thou eatest thereof thou shalt surely die."* God's commandments are not optional. When we disobey, there is a price to be paid. Romans 6:23, *"For the wages of sin is death."* God let Adam know that if he disobeyed the commandment of the Lord, death would follow. This was not just physical death that man would now be subject to, but a dying of innocence, a rejection of all that is holy, a banishment from his presence.

We see the word of God being given to Adam verbally. These words were initially spoken to Adam before the creation of Eve; it now becomes the responsibility of Adam to communicate this message to His wife and children. Any time you repeat words from another conversation, they can be called into question. Even though Adam was undoubtedly faithful in giving Eve the exact words of God, when Satan shows up, notice with whom he starts talking and his tactic of attack. He approaches Eve. Remember, it was not recorded that Eve was present to hear the Lord speak to Adam concerning the Tree of Knowledge. It could have been that everything she believes relies on; what Adam has told her God said. The temptation begins with, has it been communicated correctly? Was the words simply Adam's version of God's words? Or, in the words of Satan, Hath God said?

Eve had to have faith that the word she received from Adam was indeed the Word of God. We must hold this same faith today. There is historical and archaeological proof that God's Word is inerrant. But if no historical records existed, if no artifacts had ever been discovered, we must have faith that the Word of God is without error.

She seems to have held this faith initially, but Satan would soon meet her on the battlefield. This was the first recorded battle in human history, and it was waged over the words of God. The devil knew it would be in Eve's life if he had any chance of deception.

The tactic that Satan chose was to quote God's words but to leave out or take away from what he said, thus changing the meaning of the words. He quoted, ***"Yea, hath God said, Ye, shall not eat of every tree of the garden?"*** He, however, left out, ***"But of the tree of the knowledge of good and evil, thou shalt not eat of it."*** By doing this, he is putting a question mark in her mind. Does God contradict himself? Does God mean what he says? Critics of God's word often misquote or take scriptures out of context to dispute the validity of God's Word. Since there was no written word then, Eve had to rely on her memory of the communication she had received from Adam.

Just as it was wrong for Satan to take away from God's word, it was also wrong for Eve to add to

God's word. Notice her response to the serpent, Genesis 3:2,3,

> *"And the woman said unto the serpent, We may eat of the fruit of the trees of the garden: But of the fruit of the tree, which is in the midst of the garden, God hath said, Ye shall not eat of it, neither shall ye touch it, lest ye die."*

God did not say, do not touch it! She created a stipulation that God had not required. Satan immediately latched on to this and encouraged her to look at the tree more closely.

Genesis 3:4-6,

> *"And the serpent said unto the woman, Ye shall not surely die: For God doth know that in the day ye eat thereof, then your eyes shall be opened, and ye shall be as gods, knowing good and evil. And when the woman saw that the tree was good for food, and that it was pleasant to the eyes, and a tree to be desired to make one wise, she took of the fruit thereof, and did eat, and gave also unto her husband with her; and he did eat."*

Now, notice this act of looking toward the tree. It encompasses every aspect of temptation. I John 2:16 says,

> *"For all that is in the world, the lust of the flesh, and the lust of the eyes, and the*

pride of life, is not of the Father, but is of the world."

She saw it was pleasant to the eye, the lust of the eye. She saw it was good for food, the lust of the flesh. And she saw it would make one wise, the pride of life.

The temptation to sin does not begin with a passing glance but with an examination. The *Strong's Exhaustive Concordance* defines the word saw in this text as: consider, discern, or advise self. Eve steps closer and stares intently. The words of Satan rang in her ear, **"Hath God said."**

Next, she took it. She touched it, and nothing happened. This is why it is detrimental to our souls to add to the words of God. Once she touched it, God's other commandments were called into question. Let us look at what Jesus said about changing God's word: Rev. 22:18,19,

> *"For I testify unto every man that heareth the words of the prophecy of this book, If any man shall add unto these things, God shall add unto him the plagues that are written in this book. And if any man shall take away from the words of the book of this prophecy, God shall take away his part out of the book of life, and out of the holy city, and from the things which are written in this book."*

While we readily agree that taking away from God's words is wrong, be careful never to add to them.

People have created commandments of themselves that they were not able to follow, and their faith has been made shipwreck.

She ate it. She has now disobeyed God's commandment. The Bible says in I Timothy 2:14,

> *"And Adam was not deceived, but the woman being deceived was in the transgression."*

The devil deceived Eve. The first sin ever committed is rooted in misquoting and revising God's Word. Therefore, it is critical to have a bible that is a translation of God's Word and not just a revision of God's Word.

She gave it to Adam. Misery loves company. Adam was not deceived. He knowingly disobeyed God's commandment. When Adam took this fruit and began to eat it, there was never a time that he thought it was pleasing to God. He knew the commandments; he heard them for himself. Adam partook with full knowledge that it was a transgression against God's commandments. Through this blatant act, sin entered into the world, Rom. 5:12,

> *"Wherefore, as by one man sin entered into the world, and death by sin; and so, death passed upon all men, for that all have sinned."*

The spoken word is still powerful and holds an intricate part in God's communication with his people today. Eph. 4:11 says,

"And he gave some, apostles; and some, prophets; and some, pastors and teachers;"

These are all positions that are ordained by God for the edifying of the body of Christ.

Paul said in I Corinthians 2:4,

"And my speech and my preaching was not with enticing words of man's wisdom, but in demonstration of the Spirit and of power."

Through the Spirit's gifts, God speaks directly to his people. A gift of a word of knowledge, a gift of a word of wisdom, divers kinds of tongues, interpretation of tongues, and prophecies, all of these are ways that God continues to speak verbally to his people.

We know that just as surely as God spoke in times past through the Holy men of Old, he continues to speak to his people today through the Holy Ghost.

Let me, however, leave you with a sobering thought. Paul revealed the seriousness of proclaiming the gospel and the repercussions of changing God's spoken Word. He said in Gal. 1:8-9,

But though we, or an angel from heaven, preach any other gospel unto you than that which we have preached unto you, let him be accursed. *As we said before, so say I now again, If any man preach any other gospel unto you than that ye have received, let him be accursed."*

If anyone hears from God, their words will not contradict God's written Word. If their preaching or teaching does not agree with the Bible, they should not be received.

Written Communication

Why is writing so powerful? Writing takes ideas and makes them more concrete for us. We can meditate on them, understand them, and allow them to affect our lives. We can read instructions repeatedly to ensure we do a task correctly. We can repeatedly read notes of love and inspiration to lift our spirits. We can examine a contract to ensure the terms are followed. The written word cannot be misunderstood or disputed as quickly as a verbal conversation. And when passed from one generation to another, it will remain the same.

God knew man needed a written word. One that would be inerrant, a book that God inspired. Inspiration is a term found in the Bible which expresses the truth that the Bible is God's Word. 2 Tim. 3:16,

> ***"All scripture is given by inspiration of God**, and is profitable for doctrine, for re-proof, for correction, for instruction in righteousness."*

The word inspiration can be interpreted as God-breathed. This God-breathed book would be a perfect guide. While God dictated portions of scriptures, the Holy Ghost moved on the writers so that the words they wrote were not by their will but inspired by God.

2 Peter 1:21

For the prophecy came not in old time by the will of man: but holy men of God spake as they were moved by the Holy Ghost.

God planned that his word would be kept intact. The word intact comes from the Latin *intactus*, meaning not touched. His Word is preserved for every generation. Pastor (Dr.) D A Waite wrote,

> "In a special sense, the Bible is a timeless book. That is, it will never have an end. It will never cease to exist. There will never be a year or a century, either now or in the future, when it can be accurately said; The Bible is no more. It has disappeared. It has evaporated." *1

The first five books of the Bible are referred to as the Pentateuch. The following passages in the Pentateuch mention that Moses wrote things down often at God's direction.

Ex. 17:14,

*"And the **Lord** said unto Moses, Write this for a memorial in a book, and rehearse it in the ears of Joshua: for I will utterly put out the remembrance of Amalek from under heaven."*

Ex. 24:3-4,

"And Moses came and told the people all the words of the Lord, and all the

> *judgments: and all the people answered with one voice, and said, All the words which the Lord hath said will we do. And Moses wrote all the words of the Lord, and rose up early in the morning, and builded an altar under the hill, and twelve pillars, according to the twelve tribes of Israel."*

Num. 33:2,

> *"And Moses wrote their goings out according to their journeys by the commandment of the **Lord**: and these are their journeys according to their goings out."*

Deut. 31:24,

> *"And it came to pass, when Moses had made an end of writing the words of this law in a book, until they were finished."*

Jewish tradition attributes the authorship of the majority of the Pentateuch to Moses. There are also references in the Bible mentioning the book of the law of Moses or the book of Moses. Joshua 1:7-8, 2 Chr. 25:4, Neh. 13:1. Jesus attributed the authorship to Moses. Mark 7:10,

> *"For Moses said, Honour thy father and thy mother; and, Whoso curseth father or mother, let him die the death:"*

Moses wrote down the words of the law God gave him, as God instructed. This ensured that everyone knew exactly what God required of his people. They knew the promises, as well as the curses, associated with the keeping or breaking of the law. The written commandments were encouraging, powerful, and undeniable.

To demonstrate the power of the Word of God, as it had been written in the Old Testament, Jesus quoted the Old Testament scripture to Satan. After fasting for 40 days, Satan approached Jesus and hurled three darts of temptation toward him in the wilderness. Each time Jesus responded by saying, *"it is written,"* then quoted an Old Testament verse to soundly defeat the Devil (Matthew 4:1-11).

The written word should be read and studied faithfully. While it is commendable and advisable to commit Scripture to memory, one should only rely on their memory partially. I have heard many people misquote the Bible unintentionally. When sharing it with someone, do not just quote it; give them the chapter and verse so they can read it for themselves.

LANGUAGE

Old Testament Written in Hebrew

From the time of creation until after the flood in Genesis, the whole earth was of one language. In Genesis 11:1-9, the Bible tells of the construction of the Tower of Babel. Chapter 11, verse one says, *"the whole earth was of one language and of one speech."* The Lord saw that man had unified, not to worship and serve the Lord, but to make a name for himself; nothing would be restrained in all he imagined. Verse number seven says, ***"Let us go down, and there confound their language, that they may not understand one another's speech."*** God confounded the languages and scattered humanity upon the face of the whole earth. Because of this event, various languages were created by man out of necessity.

The Hebrew people were first mentioned after the scattering of the people at the tower of Babel. Abraham was the first person in the Bible to be referred to as Hebrew. Gen. 14:13,

> *"And there came one that had escaped and told Abram the Hebrew."*

It would be reasonable to infer that the native language of Abraham was Aramaic since he migrated from Ur of the Chaldees to the land of Canaan. Aramaic and Hebrew are closely related with quite similar terminology. It is commonly accepted that it was during Abraham's lifetime that the Hebrew alphabet was created, and Hebrew became the official language of the Hebrew people. Since the Hebrew nation was God's chosen people, the Old Testament would be written in Hebrew. The only exception was two portions of scripture found in Daniel 2:4-7:28 and Ezra 4:8-6:18. These verses were written in Aramaic. Aramaic was the language of the Persian empire and, as mentioned earlier, was remarkably similar to the Hebrew language. *2

The Paleo-Hebrew script also referred to as Old Hebrew, is the writing system found in Canaanite inscriptions from the region of biblical Israel and

Judah. It is considered the script used to record the original texts of the Hebrew Bible. *3

Paleo-Hebrew consisted of twenty-two letters. This square script was often carved on stone tablets and cave walls. The earliest inscription in Paleo-Hebrew script is the Zayit Stone discovered on a wall at Tel Zayit in Beth Guvrin Valley in the lowlands of ancient Judea. *4

As writing material evolved from stone to Papyrus, the Paleo-Hebrew script also began to change. The letters progressed from a square script to a script easier to inscribe with a stylus or quill.

Historically, two scripts have been used to write Hebrew: the Paleo-Hebrew and the traditional Jewish script. In the traditional form, the Hebrew alphabet is an abjad consisting only of consonants, written from right to left. It has twenty-two letters, five of which use different forms at the end of a word.

Sizeable portions of the Old Testament were written in Hebrew verse. Hebrew verse requires a parallelism of statement. Each statement must be presented two or three times in different words or from a different angle by repetition or contrast. How much force the Hebrew language can transmit, vigor, color, tone, and beauty is utterly unique. It would often take two or three English words to correctly translate a single Hebrew word. *5

New Testament is Written in Greek

Hebrew was the language of the Jewish people, while the Old Testament was written. However, Alexander the Great swept through Palestine on his conquests between the close of the Old Testament and the birth of Christ. In his campaign to spread Greek culture to the world, he established Greek as the language of trade. By the time of the New Testament Church in the first century AD, Greek culture had greatly influenced and changed the people and culture of Judea. Greek, not Hebrew, was the commonly used language of the Mediterranean world during the rule of the Roman Empire. It remained the dominant language, especially in the large cities of Alexandria and Antioch, until after the Arab Muslim conquest, long after the Western Roman Empire fell in 476 A.D.

Since most people understood Greek, it was the language most suitable for spreading the gospel message. The New Testament authors wrote in Greek to assure a more comprehensive understanding, though they most likely were literate in Hebrew. Paul, who was known as the apostle to the gentiles, could travel everywhere and be understood while speaking Greek.

The well-known Jewish historian of the New Testament period, Josephus, stated that the ability to speak Greek was quite common not only among the general populous but also among servants and enslaved people.

Writing material

First, it had to be determined on what material the words would be written. The following chronologically highlights this material from the writing of the original scriptures until the King James Bible was published in 1611.

The earliest material that was used was stone. In Ex. 32:15-16, it was recorded that God himself wrote two tables of testimony, tables of stone. Moses brings these down from the mount, but when Moses saw the people had constructed a molten idol god, he cast the tablets down and broke them to pieces.

Another material that was used was clay tablets. Characters were inscribed or jabbed into the clay while it was still soft. The clay tablets were then dried or baked and stored on shelves. Thousands of such tablets have been unearthed by archeologists. These were found to be durable and much lighter than stone.

In the beginning, Papyrus was used most frequently because of its availability, and it was easy to work with, but it was not durable and would give way to parchment in time. Papyrus was made from the pith of the reed plant. It was cut into strips about a foot long, placed on a flat surface, and glued together crossways like a plyboard. When dried, the whitish surface was polished smooth with a stone. The fibers ran horizontally on the front side and the back side vertically. Since the front side was smoother than the back, one typically wrote only on the front side.

Although single sheets of papyrus served various purposes, longer documents demanded that sheets of papyrus be spliced together to form a roll. Papyrus sheets were thicker than modern paper but could easily be rolled. Rolls up to thirty feet were not at all uncommon. They were usually rolled around a stick called a navel. The writing in these rolls of papyrus was in columns. This roll or scroll was called a book. *6

The following writing material was parchment. Parchment would become the writing material of choice for several hundred years. Whereas Papyrus is made from plants, parchment is made from animal skin. The skins would be soaked in limewater, and the hair on one side and the flesh on the other would be removed. The skin would then be stretched, dried, and smoothed with a pumice stone. Parchment was durable and could even be erased and written on again. To begin with, parchment was in the form of scrolls, but eventually, the parchment codex (book form) prevailed over the scroll. Both sides of the parchment could be used for writing in the codex form. Most of our manuscripts of the Old Testament and the New Testament are parchment codices. The most desired parchment was made from young calves and was called vellum. *6

Paper, a thin non-woven material traditionally made from milled plant fibers, was first documented in 25-220 AD. The milled plant fibers would be ground to powder, mixed with water, rolled out in sheets, and hung to dry. This paper-making process was brought to Europe in the 11th century and would soon replace animal skin-based parchments. By 1611 the process of making paper had advanced to such a place that paper mills had come into existence. *7

Writing Tools

A writer needed not only material to write on but also instruments with which to write.

A chisel would be needed for writing or engraving on stones and cave walls. This is one reason that the Paleo-Hebrew script was a block script. The chisel could quickly and consistently engrave these block letters on stone or wood.

Soft clay would require a stylus of wood or bone. These styluses allowed more curvature to the letters and tremendously sped up the writing process.

A pen would be needed for writing on papyrus, parchment, or paper. The earliest pens were made from a reed plant. By splitting the point of the reed, it would form a nib.

Writing Fluid

And lastly, a writing fluid would be needed. Black ink would be made from soot mixed with a gum material. This would be dried into cakes and then moistened with water when ready to use. *8

According to H. S. Miller, there were eight rules that the Jews used for the copying of the Synagogue Rolls of the Old Testament. The third rule states,

"The ink must be of no other color than black, and it must be prepared according to a special recipe." These rules are mentioned in the Talmud. *9

The Talmud contains the Jewish civil and ceremonial laws.

In summary, God's word to man started with a verbal conversation and then moved to a written form. We will explain in future chapters that God's words were written by holy men of old as they were moved on by the Holy Ghost and are the exact words that we read in the King James Translation of the Bible.

CHAPTER 2

GOD'S WORD INSPIRED

In 2 Tim. 3:16-17, the Bible reads,

"All scripture is given by inspiration of God, and is profitable for doctrine, for reproof, for correction, for instruction in righteousness: That the man of God may be perfect, throughly furnished unto all good works."

The Greek definition found in *Strong's Exhaustive Concordance* for the word inspiration, as used in 2 Tim. 3:16, means God-breathed, referring to the divine inspiration of Scripture.

Although the books of the Bible look like other ancient writings, they are inspired by God. Thus, setting them apart from all these other writings. Other writings originated from man's will, but Peter in 2 Peter 1:21 wrote concerning the prophecies that were written in the Bible,

"For the prophecy came not in old time by the will of man: but holy men of God spake as they were moved by the Holy Ghost."

The inspiration of God's Word to mankind has impressive power. It has, through the centuries, gripped the souls of men. Men who have read the Bible knew without a doubt that God was speaking to them directly. The Bible can discern the thoughts and intents of the heart. Hebrews 4: 12,

"For the word of God is quick, and powerful, and sharper than any twoedged sword, piercing even to the dividing asunder of soul and spirit, and of the joints and marrow, and is a discerner of the thoughts and intents of the heart."

The Bible is true in everything that it proclaims. The Bible includes parables, figurative language, and figures of speech, which are not intended to be interpreted literally. For example, when Jesus said, ***"I am the vine,"*** in John 15:5, he was not teaching that he was a plant. He was using figurative language to make a point. However, any time the Bible proclaims that something is true, it is true, even the miraculous, like the world's creation from nothing, the fish swallowing Jonah, and the virgin birth.

Theologians often challenge the authorship of the books of the Bible. Scoffers say, for example, that the prophet Isaiah did not author the book of Isaiah. This book of the Bible, they say, was written long after Isaiah's time. But such assertions ignore that Jesus Christ and his disciples repeatedly credit Isaiah with writing this book.—Matthew 3:3; John 12:38-41; Romans 9:27, 29.

Just before saying that God inspired the Bible, Paul told Timothy why such an inspired record was essential.

"This know also, that in the last days perilous times shall come. But evil men and seducers shall wax worse and worse,

deceiving, and being deceived." (2 Timothy 3:1,13)

In Paul's day, men were already attempting to deceive the people and weaken their faith in Jesus Christ.

I want to share a story by Jason Carlson, president of Christian Ministries International, that I recently read to illustrate the inspired Word of God.

By Jason Carlson, 5/25/11

During a question-and-answer session at a recent speaking engagement, a university student asked me, "Why do you believe that the Bible is the inspired word of God?"

In answering this student's question, I encouraged him to consider the following facts about the Bible:

First, the Bible is not just one single book. This is a more common misconception than many realize, especially with people who do not come from a Judeo-Christian background. Rather than a single book, the Bible is a collection of sixty-six books called the canon of scriptures. These sixty-six books contain a variety of genres: history, poetry, prophecy, wisdom, literature, letters, and apocalyptic, to name a few.

Second, these sixty-six books were written by fishermen, doctors, kings, shepherds, prophets, and others. And most of these authors never personally knew one another, forty different authors.

Third, these sixty-six books were written over a period of 1500 years. Yet again, this is another reminder that many of these authors never knew or collaborated in authoring these books.

Fourth, the sixty-six books of the Bible were written in three different languages. In the Bible, we have books written in the ancient languages of Hebrew, Greek, and Aramaic; a reflection of the historical and cultural circumstances in which each of these books was written.

And finally, these sixty-six books were written on three continents: Africa, Asia, and Europe. Once again, this is a testament to God's people's varied historical and cultural circumstances.

Think about the above realities: sixty-six books, written by forty different authors over 1500 years, in three different languages, on three continents. What is more, this collection of books shares a common storyline- the creation, fall, and redemption of God's people; a common theme- God's universal love for all of humanity; and a common message- salvation is available to all who repent of their sins and commit to following God with all of their heart, soul, mind, and strength. In addition to sharing these commonalities, these sixty-six books contain no historical errors or contradictions. And what is more, the Bible contains prophecies that have happened and some that are still to come.

The student's reply was almost instantaneous. He emphatically stated," But that's impossible!" It truly is impossible for any collection of human writings. However, the Bible passes this test. The Bible contains sixty-six books, written by forty different authors over 1500 years, in three different languages, on three continents, with no historical errors or contradictions. The entire Bible, from Genesis to Revelation, bears the mark of Divine inspiration. *1

The next question is being convinced that the Bible is God's inspired Word. How did God convey his message to man? Lewis Chafer said,

"The mode of divine inspiration, like many other operations of God, is not precisely defined in the Bible. Though in some instances dictation is the rule, as in the Ten Commandments, in other cases Scripture is produced without direct dictation" *2

Various portions of Scripture were dictated by God to the writers, while others were given to holy men of God as the Holy Ghost moved them. 2 Peter 1:21 states,

> *"For the prophecy came not in old time by the will of man: but holy men of God spake as they were moved by the Holy Ghost."*

The word moved in this Scripture means to bear or to carry. It is as if God handed them his words, and they took them to the people and recorded them for future generations. How he moved on them is not always clear. At other times it was through a dream or a vision, Job 33:15-16,

> *"In a dream, in a vision of the night, when deep sleep falleth upon men, in slumbering upon the bed; Then he openeth the ears of men, and sealeth their instruction."*

Sometimes it was God speaking to them through the Spirit, Ezek. 2:2,

> *"And the spirit entered into me when he spake unto me, and set me upon my feet that, I heard him that spake unto me."*

And often, it was God dealing with them to record what they saw and heard, Rev. 1:19,

> *"Write the things which thou hast seen, and the things which shall be hereafter."*

We can rest assured that every word written in the Bible was inspired by God and is, therefore, infallible. John Walvoord said, "God so supernaturally directed the writers of Scripture that without excluding their human intelligence, their individuality, their literary style, their personal feelings, or any other human factor, His own complete and coherent messages to man was recorded in perfect accuracy, the very words of Scripture bearing the authority of divine authorship." *3

If you are asked, How do you know the Bible is inspired? You should reply: The Bible contains sixty-six books, written by forty different authors, over 1500 years, in three different languages, on three continents, with no historical errors or contradictions.

CHAPTER 3

THE PRESERVATION OF GOD'S WORD

The doctrine of preservation is the teaching that God's Word has been preserved, and its original meaning has been kept intact. Psalms 12:6-7 says,

> *"The words of the Lord are pure words:*
> *as silver tried in a furnace of earth, puri-*
> *fied seven times. Thou shalt keep them,*
> *O Lord, Thou shalt preserve them from*
> *this generation forever."*

God's divine oversight has preserved God's Word from generation to generation.

I will explain the attacks that Satan has made upon God's Word and the miraculous way God has preserved it, but no amount of evidence will take the place of faith. There is an element of faith that you must possess to believe that God has preserved his Word. Heb. 11:6 says,

> *"But without faith it is impossible to*
> *please Him: for he, that cometh to God*
> *must believe that he is, and that he is a*
> *rewarder of them that diligently seek*
> *him."*

Satan has used three approaches in his endeavor to destroy the written word. The first was by destroying the physical book itself, this often-included persecution. The second was to keep people ignorant, whether through illiteracy or neglect. And thirdly, to contaminate God's Word by adding to or taking away from his Word. This last effort by Satan has led to over 350 English versions of the Bible since the King James Bible was translated.

The first tactic we will discuss is an old tactic, Satan's attempt to destroy the Bible. In Jer. 36:23, we read, "And it came to pass, that when Jehudi had read three or four leaves, he cut it with the penknife, and cast it into the fire that was on the hearth, until all the roll was consumed in the fire that was on the hearth." King Jehudi did not like God's Word and wanted to destroy the message. He thought burning the scroll leaves would do away with the message. He found out that God's Word is forever preserved. In verses 27 and 28 of the same chapter, we read, "Then the word of the Lord came to Jeremiah, after that the king had burned the roll, and the words which Baruch wrote at the mouth of Jeremiah, saying. Take thee again another roll, and write in it all the former words that were in the first roll, which Jehoiakim the king of Judah hath burned." God preserved the exact words that he had burned in the fire. As God commanded, Jeremiah re-recorded them and sent them to the king again. This demonstrated the impossibility of destroying God's Word.

Satan realizes that once someone reads the word of God, there is no silencing the message. Even though the pages be consumed with fire, one's conscience is awakened to God's truth. Satan, therefore, does not want the book to be read. Gaylord Kambarami, general secretary of the Bible Society in

Zimbabwe, Africa, knew of the power of reading the Bible.

In 1995, Gaylord Kambarami traveled to the Muriwai village to distribute copies of the New Testament. He met one man who refused to buy a New Testament. Mr. Kambarami asked him why, and he said, "Because it pollutes people." The secretary told him he would give him the Bible for free. The man said, "If you give me that New Testament, I will roll the pages and use them to make cigarettes!" Gaylord replied, "I understand that, but at least promise to read the page of the New Testament before you smoke it." When the man agreed, Gaylord gave him the New Testament.

Two years later, Gaylord Kambarami went back to the Muriwai area. He was speaking in a tent meeting, telling crowds of people how the Bible could change their lives.

Mr. Kambarami picks up the story from here: "Now, the same man I had given the New Testament to smoke was in the audience. Before the closing of the service, he stood and said, 'Please, let me say a few words. This man does not remember me; I was a drunkard when I last saw him. But he came to our village and persuaded me to take the Bible. I told him I would use the paper to roll cigarettes, but I promised to read each page before doing so, which I did. So, I smoked my way through Matthew. And I smoked the whole of Mark too. Then I smoked Luke. I started smoking John, but when I came to John 3:16, a light shone on my face. And now I am a churchgoing person. I saw the light." *1

Over the centuries, various attempts have been made to destroy God's Word. We can see Satan's hatred for the Scripture and the miraculous way God preserved his Word by examining a handful of these.

Before the canon of New Testament Scriptures was set together in one book, there was already a general sense of which books were inspired to be read and followed by Christians. In 303 AD, the Roman Emperor, Diocletian, calls for the destruction of all the scriptures of the Christians. Steve Rudd wrote, "In this year, imperial orders were given that the Christian churches were to be destroyed, the sacred books be burnt, and the clergy and all Christians be handed over for torture and be compelled to sacrifice to idols. This was the most terrifying persecution of all, producing countless martyrs." *2 So with the soldiers knocking at the door and the Christians inside, as Everett Ferguson puts it: "for the most part, they knew what books the soldiers were looking for." *3

The situation seemed to reverse under Constantine. The Roman government financed the multiplication of copies of scriptures instead of destroying them. Constantine directed Eusebius to have prepared for the churches in Constantinople fifty copies "of the sacred scriptures which you know to be especially necessary for the restoration and use in the instruction of the church." *4 Constantine's motives, however, were questionable. He required public reading in the new churches in Constantinople but from the newly sanctioned Bible, prepared by Eusebius. This Bible was based on the Alexandrian Text and was rejected by the early Christian church. Constantine was not only the ruler of Rome but became recognized as the leader of the Roman Church. He is viewed by many as the first Pope of the Catholic Church. One good thing that did come from this was the first time the books of Scriptures had been bound together in one codex. This proves that a definite canon existed between 275 and 315 AD.

Since the early Church rejected Eusebius's Bible, the original Scriptures from Antioch continued to be used by Christians. There had been copies made and distributed among the churches and the people. The New Testament Scriptures were also hidden in the catacombs during the great persecution of Diocletian. The Catacombs were a vast system of underground burial caves which proved, when needed, to be a haven for Christians. These were used on and off until 313 AD when Christianity was legalized, and Christians were allowed to have funerals above ground.

There was a long period when men were forbidden to read the Bible. Not only to read the Bible but even to possess a Bible. The Council of Tarragona 1234, in its second canon, ruled that: "no one may possess the books of the Old and New Testament in the Roman language, and if anyone possesses them, he must turn them over to the local bishop within eight days after the promulgation of this decree, so that they may be burned..." *5

David W. Cloud wrote of the Catholic Church's attempt to destroy the Bible.

"For six hundred years, the Roman Catholic Church attempted to keep translations of the Bible out of the hands of the people. Bible-believing people were mercilessly persecuted, and their Scriptures were destroyed. Those who possessed Bibles without a license were commanded to deliver them to the Catholic authorities under the threat of inquisition terrors. Booksellers were forbidden to sell Bibles except those with a Catholic Church license. Huge quantities of Scriptures in English, German, Italian, French, Spanish, and other languages, were confiscated and destroyed throughout the 13th to the 19th centuries. Bible translators and distributors were imprisoned and burned. Even after the Catholic Inquisition was outlawed in the 18th and 19th centuries, the popes continued to condemn the free distribution of Scripture." *6

The Catholic Church wanted the Bible written only in Latin and available only to the church's priest.

Satan has tried to destroy the written Word since its conception. Even though the following is not relevant to our study of the pre-King James era, I would like to remind the reader that Satan has not ceased his endeavor to destroy the written Word of God. On November 9, 1938, in Nazi Germany, the Hitler youth held a public book burning. The Hebrew Bible had been condemned, along with several other books. The books were burned in the streets. Handwritten copies of the Torah, which were hundreds of years old, were destroyed. In Vienna, by that time, part of the Reich, Jews were chased down the street with torn Torah scrolls tied to their backs.; in Frankfort, Jews were forced to tear the Torah themselves and burn it. *7 Two hundred and sixty-seven synagogues were destroyed by fire in one night. *8 Homes were searched, and anyone found with a Bible was arrested. Over 30,000 Jews were arrested in one night. *9

Even today, Satan continues persecution in multiple countries. In March 2016, Fox News released a video from Mosul. ISIS had just driven the Christians from the city and had lit a bonfire, consuming a massive pile of Bibles and other Christian literature. *10

The United Nations says that there are 198 countries in the world. The Bible is outlawed or heavily restricted in fifty-two of those countries. In fifteen of these countries, bibles can only be smuggled in through covert operations. In a totalitarian state in North Korea, the only thing North Koreans are permitted to worship is the nation's leader, Kim Jong-un. Bibles are banned, and those possessing one face imprisonment, torture, and even death – as do up to three generations of their family. *11

Just as God has preserved his written word from generation to generation, He will continue to preserve it in the future. In Mt. 24:35, Jesus said,

"Heaven and Earth shall pass away, but my words shall not pass away."

The second attempt the devil has used to destroy God's Word through the years is to keep people in ignorance. Satan's strategy was to keep the people from being able to obtain a copy of the Bible in their language. If they did receive a Bible, being illiterate, they would be unable to read it for themselves.

Hezser, in her book *Jewish Literacy in Roman Palestine*, claims that the total literacy in Palestine was only 3%. *12 This assumption, by Hezser, is based on an in-depth review of various writing, both by Jewish and Roman authors, from the first and second centuries. Jewish parents were responsible for educating their children, and since often the parents could not read or write, they taught them to memorize portions of the Torah. Their education consisted of a thorough knowledge of Mosaic History. *13

Rome was a republic that conquered Italy in 200 BC and, over the next two centuries, would conquer Greece, Spain, the North African Coast, much of the Middle East, modern-day France, and Britain. In 27 BC, the republic would become an Empire that would endure for another four hundred years. *14 From the time it became an empire until its collapse, Rome became the world's intellectual capital. Though it made no effort to educate the Jews, it opened schools and began educating Roman citizens. At the peak of Greek civilization, about one-third of the adult popula verbal equivalence tion could read and write. *15

However, in 476 AD, the last Roman emperor was defeated, and Rome fell into disarray. All gains toward literacy would be quickly lost.

When Rome fell, the world began an era known as the Dark Ages. It was characterized by economic, intellectual, and cultural decline. It would last one thousand years. While Rome as an empire had fallen, another giant rose during the Dark Ages, the Roman Catholic Church. The Catholic Church realized that the Bible was the most dangerous weapon that could be used against them. Therefore, they sought to keep people illiterate and prohibit them from accessing a Bible in their language. Since the Catholic Church's Bible was in Latin and was limited to who could access it, the priest would be the only one to read and interpret the Bible. This would lead to false doctrines and deceptions.

However, in those early years, men like Bishop Alexander, and Bishop Donatus, rose from within the ranks of the Church and condemned the Church for its teachings on the sacrament and infant baptism. To keep the world in ignorance, this era would become known for the Crusades, the Inquisitions, the Great Schism, and the martyrdom of Christians. But God preserved his Word through all these attacks.

The Renaissance era began in 1400 AD. This era was characterized by an effort to revive and surpass the ideas and achievements of the past. It is estimated that between 1500 AD and 1700 AD, the literacy rate increased from sixteen percent to fifty-three percent in western Europe. *16 This increase in literacy created a demand to have the Word of God translated into English. The King James translation would be a result of that desire. Regarding literacy, in the Renaissance era, men strived for correctness and intelligence.

Today, Satan continues to strive to keep people in ignorance. It is not through illiteracy but through neglect. The Bible is covered with dust, and a generation has risen that knows more about sports, gaming, fashion, and entertainment than they know about God's Word. Some are ignorant because they cannot read, and others are ignorant because they will not read.

Lastly, the Devil has sought to destroy the Bible by changing the Word of God. As I have mentioned, this was Satan's tactic in the Garden of Eden when he made his first assault on Eve. What a clever and deceitful idea. Do not take away God's Word but corrupt it and cause it to be altered so that it no longer contains the Words of Life. Rev. 22:18,19,

> *"For I testify unto every man that heareth the words of the prophecy of this book, If any man shall add unto these things, God shall add unto him the plagues that are written in this book. And if any man shall take away from the words of the book of this prophecy, God shall take away his part out of the book of life, and out of the holy city, and from the things which are written in this book."*

Verbal Equivalence

The King James Bible translators used what is called verbal equivalence. This means they desired to take a word from Hebrew or Greek and translate it into English with a word that meant the same thing. A word-for-word translation. The various revised versions of the Bible do not use verbal equivalence but dynamic equivalence. Dynamic equivalence permits them to add, subtract, change, or omit God's Word.

It is essential to keep the Word of God intact. According to Mt. 5:18,

"Till heaven and earth pass, one jot or one tittle shall in no wise pass from the law, till all be fulfilled."

The word intact means not damaged or impaired in any way: complete, unharmed, unaltered. The ultimate desire of the men who translated the King James Bible into English was to keep God's Word intact and every jot and tittle in place.

A jot is the tenth letter in the Hebrew alphabet and the smallest. It is written above the line and looks to us like an apostrophe. A tittle is even smaller than a jot. A tittle is a letter extension, a pen stroke that can differentiate one Hebrew letter from another. An example can be seen in the comparison between the Hebrew letters resh and dalet.

The resh, on the left, is made with one smooth stroke. The dalet on the right is made with two pen strokes. The letters are similar, but the distinguishing mark of the dalet is the small extension (the tittle) of the roof of the letter.

Jesus was stating emphatically that God's Word is true and trustworthy. God has spoken, his words have been written down accurately, and what He said will indeed happen. Even the smallest letter will be fulfilled. Even the most minor pen stroke will be accomplished. Do not accept a revision of God's Word when you can have the Word in its entirety.

We will mention more on this subject in future chapters. But, for this chapter, I want to point out that even though there has been significant effort by Satan to change God's Word, it came to King James and his translators in an unaltered state. God preserved it.

CHAPTER 4

THE PROCESS OF PRESERVATION

The history of how the Bible has been preserved is genuinely miraculous and inspiring. From its beginning, God saw to its protection. Although we do not know much about ancient times, Jewish tradition tells us that Noah, the tenth generation from Adam, preserved and protected the genealogical records given to us in Genesis five. One of two things took place. Either Noah received and carried the Genesis account of creation, the genealogical records, and all other Sacred writings into the ark, or God himself revealed these things to Moses. The first explanation appeals to our intellectual reasoning. The last plausible way mentioned would require faith, but no more faith than it would believe every verse in the Bible is God-breathed.

The first record of the charge to protect the Scriptures appears at the time of Moses. We read in Deut. 31:24-26, that Moses charged the Levites with this task,

> *"And it came to pass, when Moses had made an end of writing the words of this law in a book, until they were finished, That Moses commanded the Levites, which bare the ark of the covenant of the LORD, saying, Take this book of the law, and put it in the side of the ark of the covenant of the LORD your God, that it may be there for a witness against thee."*

Moses commanded the Levites to keep the book of the law, which He had written, inside the Ark of the Covenant. This demonstrated to the people of Israel that the Word of God should be guarded and respected.

King Josiah of Judah played a significant role in preserving the Old Testament. His grandfather Manasseh, king of Judah, turned the people entirely away from God and God's Word. In the eighteenth year of King Josiah's reign, a book of the law was found in the Temple (2 Kings 22:8-13). Hilkiah, the priest, gave the Book to Shaphan, the scribe, and Shaphan read the Book of the Law to the king. Josiah was thunderstruck by what he heard. He realized that the wrath of the Lord was kindled against them because they had failed to live by God's commandments. Josiah set about to make a significant reform in the land. He eliminated idolatry from Jerusalem and Judah. He knew that to spare the nation from the judgment of God; He must rehearse all the words of the book in the ears of the people. He did not change it but read it as it had been written. The Bible spoke of King Josiah in this manner, 2 Kings 23:25,

> *"And like unto him was there no king before him, that turned to the LORD with all his heart, and with all his soul, and with all his might, according to all the law of Moses; neither after him arose there any like him."*

Notice what Clarke's Commentary says about Josiah: "And if the king and the high priest, who were both men of eminent piety, were without this part of the Holy Scripture, it can scarcely be thought that anyone else then had it. But a religious prince like King Josiah could not leave this long unremedied. By his order, copies were written out from this original; and search being made for all the other parts of Holy Scripture … and thenceforth copies of the whole became multiplied among the people; all those who were desirous of knowing the laws of their God, either writing them out themselves or procuring others to do it for them; … [the sacred writings] were got into private hands, who carried them with them into captivity. That Daniel had a copy with him in Babylon is certain, for he quotes the law, and makes mention of the prophecies of the prophet Jerimiah, which he could not do, had he never seen them."

The Jews were given charge over the oracles of God. According to Rom. 3:2, *"unto them were committed the oracles of God."* The Jewish scribes took it very seriously when they hand-copied the Sacred Scripture.

How Accurate were the Scribes?

The Jewish scribes held such a high regard for the Scriptures as the Word of God that they regarded copying any error as a sin. No imperfection, no matter how small, was tolerated. The successors of this meticulous scribal tradition were Jewish biblical scholars known as the Masoretes. The Masoretes developed a system of checks to ensure that every copy was as perfect as humanly possible. *1

H. S. Miller listed eight rules the Jews used in copying Synagogue Rolls of the Old Testament Scriptures. These rules are mentioned in the Talmud:

1) The parchment had to be made from the skin of a clean animal, prepared by a Jew only, and be fastened by strings from clean animals.
2) Each column must have no less than 48 or no more than 60 lines.
3) The ink must be of no other color than black and had to be prepared according to a special recipe.
4) No word nor letter could be written from memory; the scribe must have an authentic copy before him, and he had to read and pronounce each word aloud before writing it.
5) He had to reverently wipe his pen each time before writing the Word of God and wash his whole body before printing the sacred name "Jehovah!"
6) There must be a review within thirty days. One mistake on a sheet condemned the sheet; if three mistakes were found on any page, the entire manuscript was condemned.
7) Every word and every letter was counted. If a letter was omitted, an extra letter inserted, or if one letter touched another, the manuscript was condemned and destroyed at once.
8) Strict rules were given concerning forms of letters and spaces between them. *2

Rule 4 stated that no word or letter could be written from memory. The scribes must have before them an authenticated copy of the Scriptures and could not rely on their memorization ability or their knowledge of spelling when copying the Manuscript. They would pronounce the word aloud before writing it.

Rule 5 said that before penning the name Jehovah (God), the scribes would stop their work and bathe their entire body. To the scribes, this was not just a job they were elected to do but an act of worship, a fearful and wonderful privilege.

Rule 7 shows the significance that these men put on accuracy. It stated that every word and every letter must be counted, and if the count was incorrect, the manuscript was condemned and destroyed at once. According to Hebrew Made Easy, there are 419,687 words in the Hebrew Old Testament.

When these rules were followed and the copy was authenticated, it was then known as the Masoretic Text. The King James Bible was translated from the Masoretic text.

These rules may seem extreme, yet they show how sacred the Word of God was to its keepers. This gives us a firm assurance that we have the words originally inspired by God.

Until 1948, the oldest known Masoretic text manuscripts of the Old Testament that had survived were dated 895 A.D. However, in 1947, a shepherd boy discovered scrolls inside a cave northeast of the Dead Sea. These manuscripts dated between 100 B.C. and 100 A.D. Over the next decade, eleven caves were located in the surrounding area, more scrolls were found in the caves, and the discovery became known as the Dead Sea Scrolls. Every book in the Old Testament was represented in this discovery except Esther. Numerous copies of each book were discovered. For example, twenty-five copies of Deuteronomy were found, thirty copies of Psalms, and nineteen of Isaiah. The scroll of Isaiah was twenty-four ft. long. *3

Critics of the King James Bible cast doubt on the accuracy of Scripture, stating that the Old Testament was translated from a Masoretic text that was less than one hundred years old. For the Old Testament, the translators used the First Rabbinic Bible, copied by Daniel Bomberg, 1516-1517, and the Second Rabbinic Bible, copied by Ben Chayyim, 1524-1525. *4 However, the Dead Sea Scrolls were 1700 years old at the time of the King James Translation, when compared to the Masoretic text of Bomberg, agreed 95% of the time. Dr. Geisler, the author of several books on the subject of inerrancy, says the Dead Sea Scrolls provide the best external evidence showing the validity of the Masoretic Text, proving that this text type was, in fact, accurately preserved over a period of about 1,000 years from the first century to the 900s A.D. *5

The 5% variations between the two texts were all spellings of the exact words or obvious pen slips. Modern critics were proven wrong again. God's Word was shown to be accurately preserved down through the ages.

There were several other writings found along with the Dead Sea Scrolls. These were not canonized and should only be viewed as historical documents. It has been incorrectly assumed that because these scrolls were found alongside the Old Testament Scriptures, they were a new revelation, a hidden gospel. In my office, there is a copy of the King James Bible, and a few books over there is a copy of the Works of Josephus. Are they both inspired because they are on the same shelf? No, God's word is the only perfect book. If the Works of Josephus, a book of Jewish History, does not agree with the King James Bible, then Josephus was wrong. So, those who point to hidden scrolls that emerge from the Dead Sea caves as a basis for changing the Word of the Lord are deceitful, and their works are fraudulent.

The writers of the New Testament quoted from the Old Testament 320 times. It was accurate and always agreed with the original Hebrew. They never tried to change, add to it, or take away from the scriptures.

We can confidently believe that the Hebrew Text that the King James translators used in 1611 were an authenticated copy of the original Scriptures.

New Testament Preservation

Now let us look at the New Testament. The New Testament was written in Greek and consisted of twenty-seven books. These books were accepted in Antioch, the hub of the New Testament Church, as inspired by God. I will discuss the process of canonization of Scripture in the next chapter.

If we trace the manuscripts used to translate the New Testament into English back to their origins, there are only two sources: Antioch and Alexandria.

Text types representing a period or location are traceable to one of the two families of manuscripts. The name of these manuscripts was, The Majority Text, also called the Traditional Text, the Received Text, or its most common name, the Textus Receptus, which originated in Antioch, and the Minority Text, or the Critical Text, which originated in Alexandria. *6

The King James Bible uses the Majority Text to translate the New Testament from Greek into English. It can be traced back to Antioch. Antioch was the springboard of the Gentile Church. It became the center for Christians just as Jerusalem was for the Jews. Acts 11:26 says the disciples were called Christians first at Antioch. The manuscripts that Christians read in their churches were copies, if not at times the originals, of the letters and books that we know today as the New Testament. *7

W A Waite stated, in his book, *Defending the King James Bible*,

> "There are two reasons why we believe the Received Text is superior: First, it has been accepted by the churches. It has been handed down by people who knew what they were talking about. Second, it has been attested by the evidence."

The Textus Receptus includes approximately 99% of the 5,000 + manuscripts known to exist today. These manuscripts include the ones used by the King James translators and have a prominent level of agreement with each other. *8

The Minority Text or Critical Text is the basis for most modern translations, such as the NIV, NASB, RSV, Jehovah's Witness Bible, and the Catholic Bible, to name a few. It can be traced back to Alexandria. Alexandria became a city of intellectualism. It was also noted as a place where religious corruption and false doctrines were prevalent. *9 Agnostics and church fathers from Rome, Africa, and Egypt, about eighty in number, met in Alexandria to rewrite, omit, and shorten the Gospels to meet their needs. When they began to release contaminated versions of the Bible, the believers in Antioch rejected the Alexandrian Text. *10

An early version of the Minority Text was the Old Latin Vulgate. It came into existence no later than 157 A.D. The Latin version of Jerome, translated by the Roman Catholic Church order, was published in about 380 AD. Christians rejected it. The Roman Catholic Church chose the name "Vulgate" or "Common" for Jerome's translation to deceive loyal Christians into thinking that it was the true common Bible of the people. *11

The Textus Receptus is the only accurate representation of the originals we have today. Just as scribes preserved the Old Testament, the New Testament text has been preserved by believers, by faithful Christians. The New Testament was frequently read aloud and memorized by early Christians. This built a solid wall against Satan's attempts to corrupt the Word of God. Let us not underestimate the power of the Holy Ghost. The Holy Ghost is a revealer. One of the gifts of the Spirit listed in I Cor. 12:10 is the gift of discerning of spirits. When a counterfeit New Testament came into the church under the guise of God's Word or a false teacher proclaiming a new doctrine would arise, God would reveal it to be a lie.

God has always had men, whom he would call and equip, to take part in the preservation of His Word. Not only would he use men of superior intelligence, unceasing resourcefulness, and uncanny ability, but he would often use common people to complete the task of preservation. Men like you and I commit to passing down the unadulterated Word of God to our children and grandchildren. When we pass down the King James Bible to another generation and discourage using any revised Bibles, we are helping preserve the Word of the Lord.

CHAPTER 5

THE CANONIZATION OF SCRIPTURE

The Canon of the Old Testament

Canonicity is a human process of recognizing the authenticity of the Bible. The word canon was originally from the Hebrew word, meaning reed or rod. A reed was used to measure things. It came to mean anything that serves to determine or regulate. The term was applied to the authentication of the Scriptural books. A canon is the body of writings that make up God's inspired words.

In the canonization process, as the individual books were being examined, specific criteria had to be met before a book could be part of the Holy Bible. Thirty-nine books were canonized in the Old Testament.

This was only done with the use of explicit rules and standards. Dennis Leap, in an article entitled *How God Preserved the Bible*, listed four significant rules that were used to canonize a book of the Bible as Scripture:

"The first rule considers <u>divine inspiration of a book</u>. The Bible records that God specifically directed that a certain book be written. The clearest examples of this rule come from Moses and the other prophets:

> *"And the Lord said unto Moses, Write this for a memorial in a book, and rehearse it in the ears of Joshua"* (Exodus 17:14).

"And the Lord said unto Moses, Write thou these words: for after the tenor of these words I have made a covenant with thee and with Israel" (Exodus 34:27).

"Now therefore write ye this song for you, and teach it the children of Israel: put it in their mouths, that this song may be a witness for me against the children of Israel" (Deuteronomy 31:19).

God commanded Isaiah to write down the prophecies given to him. Study Isaiah 30:8.

"Now go, write it before them in a table, and note it in a book, that it may be for the time to come for ever and ever:"

This verse proves that God intended Isaiah to be read and understood far into the future. God also commanded Jeremiah to write his message in a book (Jeremiah 30:1-2; 36:1-3).

Jeremiah 30:1-2: *The word that came to Jeremiah from the LORD, saying,* **2** *Thus speaketh the LORD God of Israel, saying, Write thee all the words that I have spoken unto thee in a book.*

Jeremiah 36:1 *And it came to pass in the fourth year of Jehoiakim the son of Josiah king of Judah, that this word came unto Jeremiah from the LORD, saying, 2 Take thee a roll of a book, and write therein all the words that I have spoken unto thee against Israel, and against Judah, and against all the nations, from the day I spake unto thee, from the days of Josiah, even unto this day. 3 It may be that the house of Judah will hear all the evil which I purpose to do unto them; that they may return every man from his evil way; that I may forgive their iniquity and their sin.*

Jeremiah 36 also shows that God has a message for all nations today.

The second rule looks into <u>internal evidence within a book</u>. The book of Joshua confirms that the first five books of the law are Scripture in Joshua 1:8. The book of Judges, written by the Prophet Samuel, also confirms Moses's books as Scripture in Judges 3:1-4. Daniel confirmed that Moses's and Jeremiah's books were Scripture (Daniel 9:2, 11, 13). Peter confirmed that Paul's writings were Scripture (2 Peter 3:16).

The third rule considers <u>public action or recognition</u> of the canonization of a book. In Israel and Judah, the priests publicly read and instructed the Bible. It was Moses who began the tradition. He *commanded* the Levites to read the Scriptures to the people.

"And Moses wrote this law, and delivered it unto the priests the sons of Levi, which bare the ark of the covenant of the Lord, and unto all the elders of Israel. And Moses commanded them, saying, At the end of every seven years, in the solemnity of the year of release, in the feast of

tabernacles, when all Israel is come to appear before the Lord thy God in the place which he shall choose, thou shalt read this law before all Israel in their hearing. Gather the people together, men, and women, and children, and thy stranger that is within thy gates, that they may hear, and that they may learn, and fear the Lord your God, and observe to do all the words of this law" (Deuteronomy 31:9-12).

This public reading certified the books as Scripture.

Centuries after Moses, Ezra continued this same tradition by dutifully reading the books of the law at the Feast of Trumpets. *"And Ezra opened the book in the sight of all the people; (for he was above all the people) and when he opened it, all the people stood up"* (Nehemiah 8:5). The public reading of the Scriptures has been a tradition for millennia. Indeed, it was the case in Christ's day. He participated in the custom. *"And he came to Nazareth, where he had been brought up: and, as his custom was, he went into the synagogue on the Sabbath day, and stood up for to read"* (Luke 4:16). You should also study scriptures such as Acts 13:15 and Acts 15:21. The Jews were passionate for their traditions. Paul and the other apostles continued such customs into the true Church of God. The point here is that the people knew the Scriptures so well that it would have been impossible to read a non-canonized book in public service.

The fourth rule demands <u>consistency and accuracy in doctrine</u> within the books. The one utterly fantastic fact about the Bible is that there is no inconsistency or conflict in doctrine. One homogeneous doctrinal thread runs throughout the Bible from Genesis through Revelation. This fact alone demonstrates that one divine mind orchestrated the writing of the Bible." *1

Dr. Ernest L. Martin has been recognized as one of the leading scholars and authorities on the canonization of the Bible. In his book *Restoring the Original Bible*, using Scripture as evidence, Martin notes that five periods are relevant to the canonization of the Old Testament: 1) Moses' time, 2) the reigns of David and Solomon, 3) the revival period under Hezekiah, 4) the time just before and during the exile (beginning with the reforms of Josiah), and 5) the post-exilic period under Ezra and Nehemiah. *2

In *Getting Acquainted with the Bible*, Martin Hegland writes:

> "There is much evidence to indicate that the canon of the Old Testament was fixed by about the year 400 BC, largely as a result of the work of Ezra, Nehemiah, and a council of Jews known as the Great Synagogue... long before that time, however, many of the books we now have in the Old Testament had been agreed upon as inspired" *3

These copies remained intact until Titus destroyed the Temple in 70 A.D. All the synagogues in the first century maintained the same canon of Scripture. All scrolls agreed with the divine canon.

Jesus Christ canonized the Old Testament just after His resurrection. He told his disciples in Luke 24:44,

> *"These are the words which I spake unto you, while I was yet with you, that all things must be fulfilled, which were written in the law of Moses, and in the Prophets, and in the Psalms, concerning me."*

The Canon of the New Testament

By the end of the first century AD, all twenty-seven documents that constitute the New Testament were written and circulating among early Christians. However, it was not until later that these texts were collectively named the New Testament.

For a document to become canonized as part of the New Testament, first, there had to be the actual use of these writings by early Christian authors. By noting the frequency and manner of their citations by church leaders. Second, there must be provenance relating to the authority of the document. And finally, the contents and arrangements must be consistent and in agreement with all other canonized Scriptures.

Even though, according to Unger, 397 AD is considered the official canonization of the New Testament, The third Council of Carthage ratified it, *4 this Latin translation was based on the Alexandrian Text and was viewed as corrupt. The church already accepted the books they chose but the changes made while translating to Latin were unacceptable. Acceptance of the theory of an extended period of canonization opened the door for the Roman Catholic Church to claim that other writings should be included as canonized scripture.

Martin states: "The New Testament itself speaks about its canonization….It was the apostles themselves who put together the New Testament books, not an unknown church group or groups of the second and third or fourth centuries" *5

The nineteenth-century German scholar Theodor Zahn also concluded that the canonization of the New Testament was set by the end of the first century. Harry Y. Gamble wrote this summary: "Zahn's massive study of the history of the canon ... argued that there was already a canon of Christian Scriptures by about the end of the first century (80-110 AD). There had arisen a body of Christian documents read in public worship and universally recognized and cited. They comprised the fourfold Gospel, the thirteen Pauline letters, and other writings. Zahn believed that this was documented by the fact that the church fathers, especially the early second-century Apostolic Fathers, were fully aware of these texts, which they took as fundamental resources of the church at large." *6

The Apocrypha has not been Canonized

The Old and New Testament contains sixty-six books and is considered the Scripture canon. However,

I would like to discuss another grouping of books called the Apocrypha. The Apocrypha consists of fourteen books. They are ancient religious documents that the early Church did not canonize. Even though these books existed before the time of the apostles, they were never referred to or quoted throughout the New Testament. In contrast, the Old Testament is quoted over 250 times in the New Testament.

The Apocrypha was supposedly written for 400 years, stretching from Malachi until the second century AD. This era has been called the silent years because God did not speak to his people through a prophet. When these books mysteriously emerged, the Rome Church Fathers claimed they were so divine they had hidden them away for their protection. The Oxford Dictionary defines Apocrypha in this manner, works, usually written, of unknown authorship or doubtful origin. *7 The word apocryphal was first applied to writings kept secret because they were the vehicles of knowledge considered too profound or too sacred to be disclosed to anyone other than the initiated. Apocrypha was later applied to writings that were hidden not because of their divinity but because of their questionable value to the church. In typical use, the word Apocrypha has come to mean "false, spurious, bad, or heretical."

According to Herman Hoeh,

"The addition of Apocryphal books to the
Old Testament did not begin until about
80 AD. Numerous books were gradually

introduced into the inspired canon. No two copies of the earliest Catholic Bibles agree as to which Apocryphal books were added. It was not until 397 AD., at the council of Carthage, that Augustine led the council to approve seven Apocryphal books generally. The Greek Church rejected the Apocryphal books as a whole. *8

In 250 AD, a translation of the Old Testament from Hebrew into Greek was produced in Alexandria, Egypt. It was called the Septuagint. The earliest copies of the Septuagint available today contain some of these Apocryphal books. However, no copy of the Hebrew Scriptures ever contained them. Even Jerome (340-420), an early Catholic Church Father, did not believe the Apocrypha were sacred scripture. He stated,

> "As the Church reads the books of Judith and Tobit and Maccabees but does not receive them among canonical Scriptures, so also it reads Wisdom and Ecclesiasticus for the edification of the people, not for the authoritative confirmation of doctrine." *9

At the Council of Trent in 1546, the Roman Catholic Church pronounced the Apocrypha books sacred. Rome declared their authorized status as a direct response to the teachings of Martin Luther and the Protestant Reformers, who rejected these books and their teachings. *10 Many practices and doctrines of the Catholic Church are based on the Apocrypha:

prayers for the dead, the immaculate conception, the doctrine of purgatory, and salvation by penitence. Martin Luther, the reformer and founder of the Protestant movement, refuted these teachings.

The controversy and confusion come from the fact that the translators of the King James Bible placed the Apocrypha in the 1611 edition between the Old and New Testaments. The translators did not believe these books were inspired. They translated them only for their historical value. The second Cambridge Company was assigned the task of translating the Apocrypha. Alexander McClure gave the following reasons for not admitting the apocryphal books into the canon.

1. "Not one of them is in the Hebrew language, which was alone used by the inspired historians and poets of the Old Testament.

2. Not one of the writers lays any claim to inspiration.

3. These books were never acknowledged as sacred Scriptures by the Jewish Church and therefore were never sanctioned by our Lord.

4. They were not allowed a place among the sacred books during the first four centuries of the Christian Church.

5. They contain fabulous statements and statements that contradict not only the canonical Scriptures but themselves, as, in the two Books of Maccabees, Antiochus Epiphanies

is made to die three different deaths in as many separate places.

6. It inculcates doctrines at variance with the bible, such as prayers for the dead and sinless perfection.

7. It teaches immoral practices, such as lying, suicide, assassination, and magical incantation. For these and other reasons, the Apocryphal books, which are all in Greek, except one which is extant only in Latin, are valuable as ancient documents, illustrative of manners, language, opinions, and history of the East." *11

The Geneva Bible, published in Amsterdam in 1640, omitted the Apocrypha deliberately. A defense of the omission was inserted between the Testaments. This omission was in line with the prevailing tendency in England, where, in 1644, Parliament ordered that the canonical books only should be publicly read in Church. *12

The Apocrypha began to be omitted from the King James Bible in 1629. In future editions, the Apocrypha would, at times, be added and, at other times, be omitted. It was left to the discretion of the publisher and printer. Puritans and Presbyterians lobbied for the complete removal of the Apocrypha from the Bible, and in 1825, the British and Foreign Bible Society agreed, and from that time on, the Apocrypha were eliminated from all King James Bibles. *13

CHAPTER 6

THE HISTORY OF THE ENGLISH BIBLE

The English Language

The English language is relatively recent. It came into existence about 500 AD. Three Germanic tribes, the Angles, Saxons, and Jutes, from three different areas, merged into what is now known as Great Britain. These tribes spoke similar languages, and the old English or Anglo-Saxon language was born as they began to merge. By the 7th century, the Germanic language of the Anglo-Saxons became dominant in Britain. *1

By the thirteenth century, English had become the leading language in Europe. For anyone desiring to do an in-depth study on the history of the English language, David Crystal authored a book titled, The Stories of English. This British linguist focuses on the regional dialects that shape modern English language usage. Also, Donald Brake's book, A Visual History of the English Language, is a tremendous wealth of knowledge.

As the world emerged from the Dark Ages and began to enter the Renaissance period. There was an emphasis placed on education and literacy. Europe became the gathering place for intellectuals, and English became the prominent language of the day.

Early English Translations

The first known translation of an actual biblical text in Old English was a work on the Psalms by Aldhelm, a bishop of Sherborne in Dorset. It began sometime at the beginning of the eighth century. *2

The Venerable Bede, an English monk and great scholar of his day, translated the Gospel of John. Tradition records his task completion at the very hour he lay dying. Unfortunately, his work has not survived. *2

The tenth-century translation of the four Gospels into old English, known as the Wessex Gospels, is the first extended portion of the Bible into English. The Wessex Gospels are anonymous and do not bear a date. The earliest known manuscript dates from the 12th century. *3

Copies of the Bible, for the common people were not available. They were either not in the laity's language, too scarce to locate, or intentionally withheld. The notion of the day was that only the clergy could own, read, and correctly interpret the Scriptures. The use of the Bible by the poor was not possible until the end of the fourteenth century. *4

John Wycliffe

John Wycliffe is one of the most recognized names in the history of Bible translations. The first complete Bible manuscript in English was produced in 1380 AD by John Wycliffe, an Oxford professor, scholar, and theologian. He is called the "Morning Star of the Reformation."

John Wycliffe was admitted as a student at Queen's College, Oxford, but soon moved to Merton College, the oldest, wealthiest, and most famous of the Oxford colleges. It is supposed that he was privileged to attend the lectures of Thomas Bradwardine and that from his works, he derived his first views of the freeness of grace and the utter worthlessness of all human merit in the matter of salvation. *5 Wycliffe secured his Doctor of Divinity degree in 1372 and immediately became a leading professor at the university. *6

Wycliffe was well known throughout Europe for his opposition to the various teachings of the Catholic Church, of which he was a part. He believed that teachings such as purgatory, transubstantiation, the priesthood, and private confession of sins were contrary to the Bible. By directly denying the prevailing ideas of the Catholic Church, he aroused intense opposition. He taught that the Bible was the Word of God and that no doctrine, human tradition, or any of the ordinances of the church should prevail over God's Word. He viewed the church not as the visible Catholic Church but as Christ's body, consisting of the whole number of the elect. *7

John Wycliffe believed that every believer should strive to understand the Bible for themselves and have a Bible in their language. He said, "Christ taught his followers in the language that was best known to them. Why should people today not do the same?" *8

With the help of his followers, called Lollards, his assistant Purvey, and other faithful scribes, Wycliffe produced dozens of English language New Testaments. Eventually, the entire Bible was translated into English by Wycliffe and his Lollards. The Wycliffe Bible was translated from the Latin Vulgate, the only source text available to Wycliffe. *9

The Roman Catholic Church was so infuriated by his teachings and translation of the Bible into English that he was in danger of martyrdom, but at 64, he succumbed to a stroke. The Lollards, however, continued copying and distributing the Scriptures. The hatred for Wycliffe and his followers increased substantially. In 1407, the Catholic Church issued a decree that restated the restrictions of English translations. The decree stated that "no man, by his authority, could translate any text of Scripture into English or any other tongue." And "if they were found guilty of this offense, they would be excommunicated and considered a heretic." The punishment was a promised death by burning the offender alive. *10

In 1415, Thirty-one years after Wycliffe died, at the Catholic Council of Constance, the Council condemned Wycliffe on 260 different counts, ordered his writings to be burned, and directed that his bones be exhumed and cast out of the consecrated ground. Thirteen years later, In 1428, at Papal command, the remains of Wycliffe were dug up and burned, and his ashes were thrown into a nearby stream. *11

John Hus and the Lollards

One of Wycliffe's followers, John Hus, actively promoted Wycliffe's ideas: that people should be permitted to read the Bible in their language and oppose the Roman Church's tyranny. Huss was forbidden to preach and was excommunicated by the Pope. Huss withdrew to the countryside toward the end of 1412. He spent the next two years in feverish literary activity, composing several treatises. The most important was The Church, which he sent to Prague to be read publicly. In it, he argued that Christ alone is the head of the church, that a pope "through ignorance and love of money" can make many mistakes, and that to rebel against an erring pope is to obey Christ.

In November 1414, the Council of Constance assembled, and Holy Roman Emperor Sigismund urged Huss to come and give an account of his doctrine. Because he was promised safe conduct and because of the importance of the council, Huss went. When he arrived, however, he was immediately arrested and imprisoned for months. Instead of a hearing, Huss was eventually hauled before the authorities in chains and asked merely to recant his views.

Hus was condemned to death in 1415 at the same assembly, the Catholic Council of Constance, at which Wycliffe had been condemned postmortem. The official sentence read, "The holy council, having God only before its eye, condemns John Huss to have been and to be a true, real, and open heretic, the disciple not of Christ but of John Wyclif." Hus was burned at the stake in 1415, with Wycliffe's manuscript Bibles used as kindling for the fire. The last words of John Hus were, "in a hundred years, God will raise up a man whose calls for reform cannot be suppressed." One hundred years later, Martin Luther appeared. In 1517, Luther nailed his famous 95 Theses of Contention into the church door at Wittenberg. The prophecy of Hus had come true!

Early in his ministry, Martin Luther, rummaging through the stacks of a library, happened upon a volume of sermons by John Huss. "I was overwhelmed with astonishment," Luther later wrote. "I could not understand for what cause they had burnt so great a man, who explained the Scriptures with so much gravity and skill." *12

The Lollards continued with the copying of the Scriptures. They also denied the authority of Rome and maintained the absolute supremacy of the word of God alone. In addition, they maintained that ministers of Christ should be poor, simple, and lead a spiritual life; and they publicly preached against the vices of the clergy. Persecution was vigorous, and during the reign of Henry V (1413-1422), sweeping measures were taken. The king was anti-Lollard and engaged in ruthless suppression.

Printing Press

It is noteworthy that in Germany, around 1450, a goldsmith, Johannes Gutenberg, invented the printing press, which started the printing revolution. Modeled on the design of existing screw presses, a single Renaissance printing press could produce up to 3600 pages per workday, compared to forty by hand-printing and just a few by hand-copying. The first book printed on the press was in 1455; it was in Latin, The Gutenberg Bible. Though 70 years later, this invention would eventually enable Tyndale to put over 50,000 copies of the English New Testament, translated from Greek, in circulation. The printing press put the Bible within reach of common people.

Desiderius Erasmus

Desiderius Erasmus was born in 1466 in Rotterdam, the second-largest city in the Netherlands. After his parents died of the plague, Erasmus was raised by monks in a monastery, where he acquired a love for books. Eventually, he left the monastery to study at the University of Paris and became a leading scholar of the 16th century. He studied ancient Greek and Latin works.

He experienced what church historian Timothy George called a "turning point" in 1504 when he discovered a century-old manuscript by Lorenzo Valla, which contained notes about Paul's Epistles based on various Greek manuscripts. Inspired by Valla, Erasmus published a critical edition of the Greek New Testament.

Erasmus collected manuscripts from all the places he could go, such as universities and monasteries. He kept these manuscripts, brought them together, and began collating them. And on March 1, 1516, he published a Greek New Testament. The translation drew from all available Greek manuscripts to compile a text with wording as close as possible to that of the original inspired Words. That work, which went through four revisions, was the first published Greek text available to the public and the first to come off a printing press.

The 1516 Greek New Testament of Erasmus focused on how corrupt and inaccurate the Latin Vulgate had become and how important it was to go back and use the original Greek language to maintain accuracy. He further believed that we should translate the scriptures into the languages of the common people, whether English, German, or any other language.

Not even Erasmus realized the significance of his accomplishment. His work became the basis for Martin Luther's German translation of the New Testament, William Tyndale's English translation, and Hungarian and Spanish translations.

A century later, Erasmus' work became the basis for the King James Version. though Erasmus never left the Roman Catholic Church, it has been said since the Reformation for five centuries, "Erasmus laid the egg that Luther hatched." *13

Tyndale's New Testament - William Tyndale

William Tyndale, a native of Gloucester, began his studies at Oxford in 1510 and later moved on to Cambridge. He holds the distinction of being the first man ever to print the New Testament in English. He was a scholar and genius, so fluent in seven languages that it was said one would think any one of them to be his native tongue.

While reading Erasmus's Greek edition of the New Testament, Tyndale realized there would be no better way to share the gospel with his countrymen than to put an English version of the New Testament into their hands. This became Tyndale's life passion, aptly summed up in the words of his mentor, Erasmus: "Christ desires his mysteries to be published abroad as widely as possible. I would that [the Gospels and the epistles of Paul] were translated into all languages, of all Christian people, and that they might be read and known." In 1523, he sought permission and funds from the bishop of London to translate the New Testament. The bishop denied his request, and further queries convinced Tyndale that the project would not be welcomed anywhere in England.

Due to widespread persecution in 1525, Tyndale fled to Germany to complete his English translation. He collaborated with Martin Luther, who was translating the bible into German at the time. Tyndale used Erasmus's Greek translation based on the original Greek and other authenticated manuscripts. David Daniell, the leading authority on the Tyndale Bible, stated that 90% of the New Testament in the King James Bible agrees with Tyndale. He began printing his Tyndale New Testaments in 1526. They were burned as soon as the Bishops could confiscate them, but copies trickled through to England. One risks death by burning if caught in the mere possession of Tyndale's forbidden books. Even with such adversity, according to Christian historian David Beale, it is estimated that upwards of 50,000 copies made it into circulation. *14

In a story related by Alexander McClure, we are shown the intense passion that Tyndale had for bible translation. McClure wrote that before he fled to Germany, Tyndale was summoned to stand before his district's priests. One who was in excellent reputation of being "quite learned" was utterly confounded by Tyndale's defense of the Scriptures. This papist, being irritated, exclaimed, "It was better for us to be without God's Law than to be without the Pope's.!" This was too much for Tyndale, who boldly replied. "I defy the Pope and all his laws, and if God spares my life, ere many years, I will cause a boy that driveth the plow to know more of the Scripture than you do!" *15

Tyndale, who had been attempting to evade arrest for eleven years, was translating the Old Testament into English. Before he completed this monumental task, he was betrayed by a man whom he had befriended, Henry Philips. He was incarcerated for precisely 500 days, then, on October 6, 1536, he was tied to a stake, strangled to death, and his body burned to ashes. Tyndale's last words were, "Oh Lord open the King of England's eyes."

What was so miraculous was that when Tyndale was uttering his dying prayer, a folio edition of his translation was printed in London by the King's printer, Thomas Berthelet. This was the first copy of Scripture ever printed on English soil. Moreover, three years later, in 1539, King Henry VIII sanctioned and funded an English Bible, the Great Bible.

Coverdale Bible – Miles Coverdale

Miles Coverdale was born in 1488 near Middleham, Yorkshire, England. He studied philosophy and theology at Cambridge University. Coverdale was most likely influenced in favor of Protestantism by Robert Barnes, an early follower of the teachings of Martin Luther. When Barnes was tried for heresy in 1526, Coverdale went to London to personally assist in preparing his defense. Coverdale opposed many of the religious practices perpetrated by the Roman Catholic church. Practices such as transubstantiation, sacramental confession, indulgences, and Purgatory. Mounting persecution and the threat of imprisonment forced him to flee to Germany.

During his exile, Miles Coverdale worked with William Tyndale and a few others on Tyndale's translation of the original languages of Hebrew, Aramaic, and Greek into English. Coverdale was one of the most influential preachers of his day, helping to lead the progress of the Reformation. His excellent German and Latin knowledge and understanding of

Greek, Hebrew, and French greatly aided Coverdale's translation work. As a result, Coverdale had a part in the publication of more editions of English Bibles in the 1500s than any other man -- his work with Tyndale on the Bible, his Psalms and Latin English New Testament, the complete Bible translation which bears his name, the Matthew Bible, the Great Bible, and a host of other publications which bear his mark or his name.

Myles Coverdale had remained a loyal disciple the last six years of Tyndale's life and carried the English Bible project forward and even accelerated it after Tyndale's death. Coverdale finished translating the Old Testament, using Luther's German text and Latin as sources, and in 1535 he printed the first complete Bible in the English language. Thus, the first complete English Bible was printed on October 4, 1535, and is known as the Coverdale Bible.

Coverdale was arrested and imprisoned by Queen Mary I (Bloody Mary). At the pleading of the King of Denmark, whom Coverdale had been acquainted with during his time in Germany, Queen Mary allowed for his deportation rather than his death. After Queen Elizabeth I took the throne, he returned to England and assumed the position of rector at St. Magnus, near London Bridge, in 1566. He died a brief time later, in 1568. *16

Matthew Bible – John Rogers

John Rogers graduated from Pembroke Hall, Cambridge, and was a rector in the City of London. He worked with William Tyndale on his translation of the

New Testament. In *Annals of the English Bible,* Christopher Anderson says that William Tyndale influenced Rogers to examine the Scriptures, which led to his conversion to Christ and his rejection of Roman Catholicism.

After Tyndale's death, Rogers published the second complete English Bible in 1537, The Mathew Bible. It was named this because he printed it under the pseudonym "Thomas Matthew." It was the first English Bible translated from the original Biblical languages of Hebrew and Greek. For Matthew's Bible, Rogers used the Tyndale New Testament and those portions of the Old Testament that Tyndale had completed (Genesis to 2 Chronicles, plus Jonah). For the rest of the Old Testament, he used copies of the original manuscripts in Hebrew, whereas Coverdale used Latin and German sources in his Old Testament translation.

Rogers returned to England in 1548 from Germany. At the ascension, in 1553, of the Roman Catholic Queen, Queen Mary I, to the throne, he preached an anti-Catholic sermon warning against "pestilent Popery, idolatry, and superstition" and was immediately placed under house arrest. In January 1554, he was imprisoned for a year. He was brought before a council in Southwark in January 1555 for examination, and within a week, he was sentenced to death by burning for heresy.

On February 4, 1555, he was burned at the stake at Smithfield in London. Rogers was offered a pardon if he would recant, but he refused. He was the first martyr under the reign of the Roman Catholic Queen Mary I, daughter of King Henry VIII.

In a book by J. C. Ryle, entitled, *Why Were the Reformers Burned?* Ryle relates to us the scene that unfolded at Roger's martyrdom:

"An immense crowd lined the street and filled every available spot in Smithfield. Until that day, men could not tell how English Reformers would behave in the face of death and could hardly believe that Prebendaries and Dignitaries would give their bodies to be burned for their religion. But when they saw John Rogers, the first martyr, walking steadily and unflinchingly into a fiery grave, the crowd's enthusiasm knew no bounds. They rent the air with thunders of applause. Even Noailles, the French Ambassador, wrote home a description of the scene and said that Rogers went to death 'as if he was walking to his wedding.' By God's great mercy, he died with comparative ease." *17

The Great Bible

In 1539, Thomas Cranmer, the Archbishop of Canterbury, hired Myles Coverdale at the bequest of King Henry VIII to publish the "Great Bible." It became the first English Bible authorized for public use.

The Great Bible, while an answer to Tyndale's prayer, was not motivated by a spiritual awaking within the heart of King Henry VIII, but rather the King was infuriated at the Church of Rome because they would not grant him an annulment of his first marriage (his first wife was unable to have a male heir and therefore the King had no heir to the throne). He struck out against the Catholic Church in two ways.

First, he renounced Roman Catholicism and took the churches of England out from under Roman control. He then assigned himself as the leader of the Churches of England, receiving not one but two marriage annulments from the church of England.

Secondly, he published an English Bible, which was blasphemy in the eyes of the Catholic Church. King Henry directed the clergy to place a copy of the Great Bible in every church. He further required it to be located where it was accessible for the parishioners to read. If they could not read, a reader would be provided for the benefit of the illiterate. It was also called the Chained Bible because it was chained to the pulpit.

The Churches of England were not Roman Catholic and were not genuinely Protestant. They became known as the Anglican Church. Because of this sudden change, some churches leaned heavily toward Catholicism in form and doctrine. And other churches that leaned strongly toward Protestantism.

Geneva Bible

From 1539 to 1553, the reformers enjoyed the freedom to continue their Bible translation work. However, in 1553, Queen Mary I began to reign in England. Queen Mary, or "Bloody Mary as she was called, was the next obstacle to printing the Bible in English. She was possessed in her quest to return England to the Roman Church. In 1555, John Rogers and Thomas Cranmer were burned at the stake. Mary went on to burn reformers at the stake by the hundreds for being a Protestant.

In the 1550s, the church in Geneva, Switzerland, was very sympathetic to the reformers and one of the only safe havens for them to continue their work. One of the blessings that came out of the persecution from Bloody Mary was a gathering in one place of some of the greatest theologians, translators, and ministers that have ever lived. Men like Myles Cloverdale, the notable translator. John Foxe, publisher of Foxe's Book of Martyrs. John Calvin, theologian and author of a complete set of bible commentaries, and John Knox, the great reformer of the Scottish Church, to name a few, were determined to produce a Bible, as well as other books, which would educate their generation and generation to come.

The Bible, created in Geneva, Switzerland, was known as the Geneva Bible. The Geneva Bible was the first Bible to add numbered verses to the chapters so that referencing specific passages would be easier. Every chapter was accompanied by extensive marginal notes and references, so thorough and complete that the Geneva Bible is considered the first English "Study Bible."

The Geneva Bible became the Bible of choice for over 100 years of English-speaking Christians. Examination of the 1611 King James Bible shows clearly that its translators were influenced much more by the Geneva Bible than any other source. The Geneva Bible contains 90% of William Tyndale's original

English translation. The Geneva Bible remained more popular than the King James Bible for decades after the King James Bible's original release. The Geneva Bible holds the honor of being the first Bible taken to America and the Bible of the Puritans and Pilgrims. The reformers safely returned to England with the end of Queen Mary's bloody reign. Queen Elizabeth allowed the printing and distribution of the Geneva Bible in England.

Bishops Bible

The institutional Church vehemently protested against the Geneva Bible's marginal notes. They felt the marginal notes were too Calvinistic in their interpretation. They desired another version that would remove these controversial notes.

The Bishops Bible was printed in 1568 and was meant to replace the Great Bible as the official Bible of England. The leading figure in translating was Matthew Parker, Archbishop of Canterbury. Despite 19 editions being printed between 1568 and 1606, it never gained a foothold of popularity among the people. The text lacked not only the notes of the Geneva Bible but also the cross-references, which were helpful to people among whom the Bible was beginning to circulate.

The translators of the King James Bible were instructed to take the 1602 edition of the Bishops' Bible as their basis, although several other existing translations were considered. After it was published in 1611, the King James Bible soon took the Bishops' Bible's place as the standard of the Church of England.

King James Bible

As the reign of Queen Elizabeth was ending, we find a draft for an act of Parliament for an updated version of the Bible: "An act for reducing of diversities of bibles now extant in the English tongue to one translated from the original." Nothing ever became of this draft during the reign of Queen Elizabeth, who died in 1603, and was succeeded by King James I.

When Queen Elizabeth I passed away, King James VI of Scotland also became King James I of England. The Protestant clergy approached the new King in 1604 and announced their desire for a new translation to replace the Bishop's Bible. They knew the Geneva Bible had won the people's hearts because of its excellent scholarship, accuracy, and exhaustive commentary. However, they did not want the controversial marginal notes. The leaders of the church desired a Bible which contained only scriptural references. Notes in the margin would consist of word clarification or cross-references but no commentary on the verses.

A conference was called by King James, the Hampton Court Conference, to address the things the Protestants felt were amiss in the Church of England. A new Bible was not on the agenda, but John Reynolds brought up the subject, and King James resolved that there might be a new translation.

Work began in July 1604 on the King James Bible. They took into consideration: The Tyndale New Testament, The Cloverdale Bible, The Matthews Bible,

The Great Bible, The Geneva Bible, The Bishop's Bible, and other various source material. These translators would consider the opinion of former translators, Bibles published in various languages, and most importantly, copies of all original manuscripts.

The King James Bible was published in 1611. In future chapters, we will discuss the journey of the King James Bible from its conception until now.

Having researched multiple sources for the contents of this chapter, I came across a website, WWW.GREATSITE.COM. This website is an online showroom of the Bible Museum. There is a page devoted to English Bible History. They sell antique Bibles and pages from the 1611 King James Bible.

CHAPTER 7

KING JAMES

An Infant King

"I never with God's grace shall do anything in private which I may not without shame proclaim upon the tops of houses." King James I, 1603

Before we examine the conception and completion of the King James Bible, let us look first at King James. Who was he? What did he believe? What part did he have in the Bible that bears his name?

James Charles Stuart was born on June 19, 1566, at Edinburg Castle in Scotland. His father, Lord Darnley, was murdered in 1567 before young James was one year old. His mother, Mary Queen of Scots, was soon forced to abandon the throne due to her suspected involvement in her husband's murder. James was crowned King James VI of Scotland at the tender age of 13 months. Reformation leader John Knox preached the sermon at his coronation. *1

Four tutors educated young James, one of the most influential was George Buchanan, a staunch Calvinist. It was under Mr. Buchanan's strict teaching methods that King James became one of the most learned and intellectual men to ever sit on any throne. Mr. Buchanan was 64 years old when he began tutoring the young king. *2

He was taught various languages, history, composition, arithmetic cosmography, dialectics, rhetoric, and theology. King James spoke fluent Greek, Latin, French, English, and Scots and was schooled in Italian and Spanish. Because of his linguistic capabilities, King James typically did not need a translator when conducting business with other heads of state.

Before James was twelve, he had taken the government into his own hands when the earl of Morton was driven from the regency in 1578.

For several years, however, James remained under the influence of the duke of Lennox. James was kidnapped by William Ruthven, 1st earl of Gowrie, in 1582 and was forced to denounce Lennox. The following year James escaped and began to pursue his policies as king. His chief purposes were to escape the influence and intimidation of the Scottish factions, which had tried to manipulate the young King, and to establish his claim to succeed the childless Elizabeth I upon the throne of England. *2

King James, The Author

King James grew into a mighty king with a powerful pen. He wrote extensively on a variety of subjects. Among his works were "a collection of the king's writings compiled by the bishop of his chapel into one volume and *"Basilicon Doron,"* kingly instruction to his eldest son. *3

In the collection of King James's writings is a pamphlet that James wrote and published titled, *A*

COUNTERBLASTE TO TOBACCO, commonly referred to as the first anti-smoking tract. Counterblaste was a strong attack against tobacco smoking. Tobacco had only recently arrived in Europe, as it originated in America, causing quite a controversy. *4

In his publication entitled, *The Meditations upon the Twenty-fifth through the Twenty-ninth verses of the Fifteenth Chapter of First Chronicles*, James uses the Biblical account of King David bringing home the ark to exhort his people to be thankful for God's deliverance from their enemies, to remain grounded in Jesus Christ alone, and to beware of hypocrites. *5

The king's writings were among their period's most important and influential writings. King James has long been known for his great learning and was known as Great Britain's Solomon even in his own time.

His Family

King James took Anne of Denmark, the daughter of Fredrick II of Denmark, to be his queen in 1859. Anne married James at the age of fourteen. King James loved his wife and wrote beautiful poetry for her. They had nine children together, three of which survived infancy: Henry Frederick, Prince of Wales, who proceeded his parents in death; Princess Elizabeth, who became Queen of Bohemia; and James's future successor, Charles I. *6

As mentioned previously, to pass on his kingly instruction to his eldest son, Prince Henry, King James wrote *Basilicon Doron,* which means "the Kingly Gift." Basilicon Doron was not meant for general publication but for the instruction of the young prince if his father would not survive to instruct him. The King bound his printer Robert Waldegrave to secrecy and ordered an edition of only seven copies. Somehow, however, the intelligence of the book and its contents got abroad. Subsequently, there was much demand for *Basilicon Doron*. The King then had it published for the general public, and it became a bestseller. It was published in English, Welsh, Latin, French, Swedish, and German for over 50 years.

Basilicon Doron consists of three short volumes, the first of which is *"A King's Christian Duetie Towards God."* He skillfully intertwines sacred scripture with godly and Christian advice.

Their eldest son, Henry, passed away in November 1612 at the age of eighteen from typhoid. Their daughter, Elizabeth, married Fredrick V, king of Bohemia, and moved away. And their only other surviving child, Charles, became King Charles I after his father's death. He reigned for 24 years, believed in the divine right of kings, and was determined to govern according to his conscience. Many of his subjects opposed his policies, particularly the levying of taxes without parliamentary consent, and perceived his actions as those of a tyrannical absolute monarch. After being defeated in a civil war, he refused to accept the terms of constitutional monarchy. Charles was tried, convicted, and executed for high treason in January 1649. The monarchy was abolished, and the Commonwealth of England was established as a republic. The monarchy was restored to Charles's son, Charles II, in 1660. *7

His Religion

The Earl of Lennox appointed George Buchanan to ensure that King James VI of Scotland was reared in the Protestant faith. By age ten, James had a good command of general knowledge and was an able student. He became one of the outstanding theologians of his day. *8

King James was not only Protestant but actually opposed the Pope and wrote vehemently against the errors of Roman Catholicism. King James knew well the spiritual and temporal dangers of Romanism. He said about praying to the virgin Mary: "And first for the blessed virgin Mary, I yield her that which the Angel Gabriel pronounced of her...I reverence her as the Mother of Christ, But I dare not mock her and blaspheme God, praying her to command and control her Son, who is her God and her Savior." *9

So influential was the King's writing against the Catholic religion that many Catholics were converted. According to the Workes, Kings across the land began to stand up and assert their right to rule their kingdoms without papal interference.

The King in Scotland and England

King James' great aspiration to be the first King of both Scotland and England was realized in 1603 upon the death of Queen Elizabeth. When Elizabeth died on 24 March 1603, as her closest relative, James was invited to become the next king of England as James I. He did have English royal blood in his veins, for James was the great-great-grandson of Henry VII of England (r. 1485-1509). When he ascended to the English throne that year, he had already been the king of Scotland for 36 years. He was now known as King James VI of Scotland & I of England.

Assassination Attempt

Roman Catholics attempted to assassinate King James in 1605 in what is known as the Gunpowder Plot. In the plot, Guy Fawkes, and other Catholics, designed a plan to blow up via gunpowder, the King, and the entire British Parliament. Fortunately, the plot was discovered before it was conducted. One of the conspirators, one Francis Tresham, sent an anonymous letter to his brother-in-law, Lord Mounteagle, who would have been present on the fateful day and was a noted Catholic peer; Mounteagle duly passed on the news of the plot, and the king was eventually informed. According to King James in his treatise entitled, "*A Catalogue of the Lies of Tortes, Together With A Brief Confutation of Them,*" it was not "just occasion of despair given to the Powder-Traitors...but the instructions which they had from the Jesuits, which caused them to attempt this bloody design." *10

The failed attempt to murder King James is remembered each year in England on November 5 and is known as Guy Fawkes Night. To celebrate the foiling of the plot, the authorities encouraged people to light bonfires on the evening of the 5th of November.

His Enemies

Besides the Catholic Church, such a man as King James was sure to have enemies. One such man, Anthony Weldon, was excluded from the King's court. Weldon was dismissed for his negative assessment of the Scots in his treatise, *A Description of Scotland*. Weldon swore vengeance. It was not until 1650, twenty-five years after the death of James, that Weldon saw his chance. He drafted a paper calling James a homosexual. James, being dead, was in no condition to defend himself. *11 The report was largely ignored since there were still enough people alive who knew it was false. It lay dormant for years until recently, when it was picked up by those who hoped that vilifying King James would tarnish the Bible that bears his name.

There are several facts to consider when addressing this accusation. First, with King James's enemies during his reign, if these rumors were true, various men would be extremely willing to publish his escapades. Secondly, King James was a family man; he was married and had nine children. He loved his wife and often composed romantic poetry for her. He spoke tenderly and lovingly of her. Thirdly, in his book, Basilicon Doron, he instructed his son; not to be effeminate, not to be guilty of adultery, and that sodomy was a terrible crime. And lastly, but most importantly, he was a Christian.

His Notable Accomplishments

The most notable accomplishment of King James was the publication of the Bible that bears his name, the King James Bible. It was also known as the Authorized Version because the king had authorized the massive undertaking. This translation was a product of a conference involving Anglicans and Puritans at Hampton Court in 1605.

In 1606, the king granted a royal charter to found colonies on the east coast of North America. In May 1607, Jamestown, named after the king, was founded in Virginia, and in 1616, Pocahontas (1596-1617), famed daughter of Chief Powhatan (1547 - 1618), traveled to England and met King James at court. In 1620 the *Mayflower* sailed for North America with the pilgrim Puritan colonists who established the Plymouth Colony. *12

The flourishing of the arts continued as they had under Queen Elizabeth. James honored William Shakespeare's acting company by granting them the title of the 'King's Men,' and many famous playwright's works, like *King Lear*, *Macbeth*, and *The Tempest*, were performed at the royal court.

His Death

Although King James had a life filled with accomplishments, he was acquainted with grief. He was a sickly man who had physical handicaps in his legs. As a result of his unsteady gait, the king had numerous falls, accidents, and injuries. He suffered from crippling arthritis, abdominal colic, gout, and kidney pain. Some believe that he may have had congenital diseases of the nervous system. Sometimes the pain was so great that the king became delirious.

The King was no stranger to pain and sorrow. The sunset on King James, the great monarch, on March 27, 1625, at Theobald Park in Herts, England. He was 58 years old when he died and was buried at Westminster Abbey. Unlike many Scottish monarchs, King James died in his bed at peace with his subjects and foreign countries. *13

CHAPTER 8

HAMPTON COURT

The Resolution at Hampton Court Conference

When the reign of Queen Elizabeth (1558-1603) was ending, we find a draft for an act of Parliament for an updated version of the Bible: "An act for reducing of diversities of bibles now extant in the English tongue to one translated from the original." The Bishop's Bible, the Great Bible, the Matthew Bible, and the Geneva Bible were all in circulation and all varied, as they had used different source material. Nothing ever became of this draft during the Reign of Queen Elizabeth, who died in 1603.

After the death of Elizabeth in 1603, James Stuart, who was already King James VI of Scotland, also became King James I of England.

One of the first things King James did, was the calling the Hampton Court Conference in January 1604. While the meeting was originally scheduled for November 1603, a plague outbreak meant it was postponed until January. The conference was called in response to a series of requests for reform, by the Puritans, in a document called the Millenary Petition, which supposedly contained the signatures of 1000 Puritan ministers. There were three meetings over a period of five days. Only four Puritan ministers were allowed to attend and present their petition. *1

The Millenary Petition requested a meeting "for the hearing, and for the determining, things pretended to be amiss in the church." Here were assembled bishops, clergymen, professors, and four Puritan theologians, to consider the complaints of the Puritans. The conference set off with a meeting between James and his bishops about some of the Puritan complaints detailed in the Millenary Petition, particularly the complaints about the Catholic terms of Absolution and Confirmation. Some practices objected to were ceremonial, such as the priest's making the sign of the cross during Baptism, the use of the ring for marriage, the rite of confirmation, and ministers' wearing of surplices. *2 The King, after ending his talks with the bishops, claimed he was "well satisfied" and declared that "the manner might be changed, and some things cleared."

Although Bible revision was not on the agenda, the Puritan President of Corpus Christi College, John Reynolds, "moved his Majesty, that there might be a new translation of the Bible, Because those which were allowed in the reign of Henry VIII, and Edward VI, were corrupt and not answerable to the truth of the Original." Accordingly, a resolution came forth: "That a translation be made of the whole Bible, as constant as can be to the original Hebrew and Greek; and this to be set out and printed, without marginal notes, and to be used in all churches of England in time of divine service." *3

The Results of the Conference

While there were many results from the Hampton Conference, we will focus only on the resolution of a new translation of the Bible. In July of the same year, King James wrote to Archbishop Bancroft that he had "appointed certain learned men, to the number of four and fifty, for the translating of the Bible." Although fifty-four were nominated, only forty-seven of the original appointees were known to have taken part in the translation work. These men were the best scholars and linguists of their day. In the preface to their completed work, it is stated that "There were many chosen, that were greater in other men's eyes than in their own, and that sought the truth rather than their own praise." According to King James, other men were sought out "so that our said intended translation may have help and furtherance of all our principal learned men within this our kingdom." *3

Fifteen General Rules

Under King James's direction, Bancroft set **fifteen general rules** for the guidance of translators. I will comment on these in detail when discussing the method used by the King James Translators, but I will submit to you these rules as found in the original folio. (edited for spelling)

Rules to be Observed in the Translation of the Bible

1. The ordinary Bible read in the church, commonly called the Bishops' Bible, is to be followed and as little altered as the truth of the original will permit.
2. The names of the prophets, and the holy writers, with the other names in the text, are to be retained as nigh as may be, accordingly, as they are vulgarly used.

3. The old ecclesiastical words are to be kept, and the word church is not to be translated into congregation.
4. When any word hath divers significations, that to be kept which hath been most commonly used by the most of the ancient fathers, being agreeable to the propriety of the place, and the analogy of faith.
5. The division of the chapters is to be altered either not at all or as little as may be if necessity so require.
6. No marginal notes at all to be affixed, but only for the explanation of the Hebrew or Greek words, which cannot without some circumlocution, so briefly and fitly be expressed in the text.
7. Such quotations of places are to be marginally set down as shall serve for the reference of one Scripture to another.
8. Every particular man of each company to take the same chapter or chapters, and having translated or amended them severally by himself, where he thinketh good, all to meet together, confer what they have done, and agree for their part what shall stand.
9. As any one company hath dispatched any one book in this manner, they shall send it to the rest to be considered seriously and judiciously; for his majesty is careful in this point.
10. If any company, upon the review of the book so sent, doubt or differ upon any place, to send them word thereof, note the place, and withal send their reasons; to which if they consent not, the difference

to be compounded at the general meeting, which is to be of the chief persons of each company, at the end of the work.

11. When any place of special obscurity is doubted of, letters to be directed by an authority to send to any learned man in the land for his judgment in such a place.

12. Letters to be sent from every Bishop to the rest of his clergy, admonishing them of this translation in hand; and to move and charge as many as being skillful in the tongues; have taken pains in that kind, to send his particular observations to the company, either at Westminster, Cambridge, or Oxford.

13. The directors in each company, to be the Deans of Westminster and Chester; for that place, and the king's professors in the Hebrew and Greek in either university.

14. These translations to be used when they agree better with the text than the Bishops' Bible: Tyndale's, Matthew's, Coverdale's, Whitechurch's [Great], Geneva.

15. Besides the said directions before mentioned, three or four of the most ancient and grave divines in either of the universities, not employed in translating, to be assigned by the vice-chancellor, upon conference with the rest of the heads, to be overseers of the translations, as well Hebrew as Greek, for the better observation of the 4th rule above specified. *4

CHAPTER 9

THE TRANSLATORS

King James approved the resolution for a new translation of the Bible and funded it, but he never translated one verse in the Bible. Even though he had an amazing knowledge of the scripture and was a proficient writer, he did not interfere with the translators or try to impose his ideas or opinions on the Bible. To clarify, the King James Bible was not translated by King James. It bears his name because he was the ruling monarch who commissioned the project.

The King appointed Richard Bancroft, Archbishop of Canterbury, as an overseer of the Bible translation project. It was Bancroft who created the 15 guidelines for translating the Bible. While Miles Smith and Thomas Bilson were the final editors of the King James Bible, Bancroft would be responsible for delivering it to the printers. I found in my research a few references to Bancroft changing 14 verses to satisfy the Anglican Church. There is, however, no reliable source for this allegation. And beside this, Bancroft died in 1610 before the Bible was published.

Though there is no record of the qualifications used to determine the candidates who would translate the Bible, a list of names was submitted and approved to King James by the Dean of Westminster and the Regius professors of Hebrew at Cambridge, Oxford, and Westminster Universities. *1 A review of the translators' lives gives us an insight into the character that was sought after, educationally, spiritually, as well as linguistically ability. As I began to study the lives of these translators, I realized it was through God's divine providence that these men were born in the same generation and could obtain such a vast knowledge of linguistics. There have been over 350 versions of the Bible in English since the King James Bible was printed. However, there has never been a group of men who have attempted to revise the Bible with the qualifications of these men. Maybe this is because these men wanted to translate the Bible, maintain its integrity, and not revise it.

All the translators were university graduates, and most held a Doctor of Divinity. All except one were ordained Church of England ministers. Five were Bishops, and two were Archbishops. They were all highly proficient in English, Hebrew, Greek, and Latin. These men were not just educated men but devoted Christians. Several had written complete commentaries on the Bible and had translated the Bible into various languages. Mile Smith, the author of the preface to the King James Bible, remarked, "they craved the assistance of God by prayer."

Every man involved in the King James Bible translation believed in the verbal inspiration of the Scriptures, all believed in the deity of our Lord Jesus Christ, and all were men of prayer.

The work began in 1604. However, the translators set the next three years aside for a time of private research, prayer, fasting, and preparation for the task ahead. The company met together in 1607 to begin the work on the translation and divided themselves into **six committees: two met at Oxford, two at Cambridge, and two at Westminster Abbey**. The Bible was distributed in **six portions among the various committees.**

Meet the Translators

Alexander McClure poured over records for twenty years to learn all he could about those who translated the Bible into English. His resulting book, *Translators Revived: Biographical Memoir of the Authors of the English Version of the Holy Bible,* stands as a monument to these dedicated Christian men. *2 The following biographical sketches are a sampling of McClure's research and will reveal these man's academic and spiritual qualifications. I also used an online source that I highly recommend, kingjamesbible-translators.org. *3 The successive academic degrees that belong to each translator could be given but will be omitted for the sake of brevity. They can, however, be examined at the website mentioned above. Besides these sources, I gleaned from the following: Gustavus S Paine's book, *The Men Behind the KJV,* Adam Nicolson's book, *God's Secretaries - The Making of the King James Bible,* and William P Grady's book, *The Final Authority – A Christians Guide to the King James Bible.*

Of the fifty-four men who were initially commissioned for the translation, only forty-seven are known to have taken part in the translation. Death and sickness plagued these men as many were well advanced in age. Eight men were brought in to fill vacancies. So, the total number of men with a commission in the translation was fifty-five. However, various other translators, pastors, theologians, professors, and linguists were brought in to advise these men in any area of concern. Some of these translators, who acted under King James's commission, are almost unknown today, though they were of high reputation in their own time. A few left us little more than a name, but their association with many scholars proves their fitness.

THE FIRST COMMITTEE

The first committee of translators was **Westminster group one**. They translated Genesis thru the Second Kings. The group consisted of ten men. Lancelot Andrews was the leader of this group.

Lancelot Andrews (Director of the 1st Westminster committee)

Lancelot Andrews was born in London in 1555. He attended Pembroke Hall, Cambridge University. Andrews was fluent in Latin, Greek, Hebrew, Chaldee, Syriac, Arabic, and at least fifteen other languages. His writings included a manual of his private daily devotions in Greek, an eight-volume set on theology, and 96 sermons. He was Dean of Westminster College for four years.

He was the leader of the Westminster group that translated Genesis thru the Second Kings. He functioned as general editor of the King James Bible.

He was a man of prayer, known to spend several hours a day in prayer. McClure stated, "if he had been present at the tower of Babel, he might have served as Interpreter-General. Andrewes had the privilege of being selected, from among all the preachers in the land, to deliver the annual Christmas Day sermon for the royal family, beginning with Queen Elizabeth and continuing for many years during the reign of King James. He was a royal Chaplain to both Queen Elizabeth and King James.

John Overall

John Overall was born in 1559. He received his Doctor of Divinity at Trinity College, Cambridge University, and was appointed Regius Professor at Cambridge University. During this time, he often preached before Queen Elizabeth I.

He had spoken in various languages so often; it was troublesome to speak English in a continued oration. Overall's writings and sermons continually exposed the Catholic Church's fraudulent activity. He began preaching that justification was obtained by repentance, this not only infuriated the Catholic Church, but the Church of England withstood him as well. He served as a Bishop in several churches; most notably, he was the Dean of St. Paul Cathedral.

Hadrian Saravia

Hadrian Saravia was a noted scholar, born in 1530; he would have been 81 years of age when the King James Bible was published. Queen Elizabeth's Council sent him as a missionary to the islands of

Guernsey and Jersey, where he was the first Protestant minister. He labored there twofold, doing the work of an evangelist and establishing a school. He published a treatise on papal primacy against the Jesuit Jacob Gretser. All his publications relating to such matters were collected into a folio edition in 1611. He was held in high esteem and held a rare skill in Hebrew learning. He would debate controversies of the time in Greek, Latin, Hebrew, and English.

Richard Clarke

Richard Clarke was born in 1564. He is spoken of as a fellow of Christ's College, Cambridge, and as a very learned clergyman and eminent preacher. He was a preacher at the church at Canterbury. Three years after his death, in 1634, a folio volume of his sermons was published.

John Laifield

John Laifield was born in 1563. He was a fellow of Trinity College in Cambridge and the rector of the Church of St. Clements, Danes, in London. It is said that he was skilled in language and an expert in biblical architecture. His judgment was as much relied on in the translation as the fabric of the tabernacle and temple. He died in 1617 at his rectory.

Robert Tighe

Robert Tighe, whose name has been misspelled, Leigh, on most printed lists of translators, was educated at Oxford and Cambridge. He was born in 1562 and was a Vicar of the Church of All Hallows,

London. He is characterized as "an excellent textuary and profound linguist." He died in 1620.

Francis Burleigh

Francis Burleigh was born in 1552. He began and completed his university studies at King's College, Cambridge, and was a Vicar of Bishop's Stratford in 1590. He held this appointment at the time he was employed in the service of translating the King James Bible.

He was one of the founders of Chelsea College, London. Chelsea was not a college, as were the colleges at Cambridge and Oxford. It had no student body per se. But instead, it was established as an institution to produce writings and lend academic support for the Reformation. Ultimately the college was dissolved in 1653, having served its purpose.

He was known to be an excellent Hebrew Scholar.

Geoffry King

Geoffry King was born in 1567 and was a fellow of King's College, Cambridge. It is a fair token of his fitness to participate in this translation work that he succeeded Mr. Spaulding, another of these translators, as Regius Professor of Hebrew at Cambridge. He was also one of the King's translators. Men were not appointed in those days to such instruction duties without ample qualifications.

He served as a personal Chaplin to King James and was a Vicar at seven different churches, most of which ministered to the lower class. He is said to have walked with royalty and ministered to the poor.

Richard Thompson

He was called the grand propagator of Arminianism, a theological movement that reacted to the Calvinist doctrine. Thomas was not alone among the translators in his Arminian leanings. John Overall and John Richardson were also believers in Arminianism, which stated that man could be saved through faith in Jesus Christ but could also reject Christ and lose salvation. Years later, John Wesley, the founder of the United Methodist Church, would become one of the most notable ministers to propagate the five points of Arminianism, though somewhat edited from Jacobus Arminius's original teachings.

Thompson brought the company a broad knowledge of available books and manuscript material and a proficiency in Hebrew, Greek, and Latin.

Richard Thompson was known for studying various languages and the communication between them. He specialized in the study of written texts and written records. Richard Montague said of him, "he is most admiral, better known in Italy, France, and Germany than at home.

William Bedwell

William Bedwell was born in 1563 and started attending college when only 15 years of age at Trinity, Cambridge. He served as the Anglican Church Rector.

He published translations of the Scriptures into Hebrew, Syriac, Chaldee, Latin, and Arabic. He produced a Persian dictionary and was compiling the manuscripts for a three-volume Arabic lexicon at the time of his death. This massive compilation of manuscripts was loaned to Cambridge University to aid in Dr. Castell's Arabic lexicon, The Lexicon Heptaglotton. He was a master of the Semitic languages, which shed much light on Hebrew words and phrases. One of his most well-known published works was *A Discovery of the Impostures of the Koran*. He denounced the Koran as an imitation Bible.

THE SECOND GROUP

The second group of King James translators was **Cambridge group one**. They were assigned from the beginning of the Chronicles to the end of the Song of Solomon. There were eight men in this group. The director of this group was Edward Lively, who died in 1605 during the translation and was replaced by Robert Spaulding.

Edward Lively (Director of 1st Cambridge committee)

Edward Lively was born in 1545. He was commemorated as one of the best linguists in the world. He was actively employed in the preliminary arrangements for the translation and stood in the high confidence of King James. He was the author of a Latin exposition of five minor prophets and a commentary on portions of the Old Testament book of Daniel. He was appointed Regius Professor of Hebrew by Queen Elizabeth I and held this position for 35 years. McClure quoted one eminent scholar who said of Lively, "Next to Pocock, he was the greatest of our Hebraists."

Lively died after four days of sickness from quinsy. (a complication from tonsillitis in which infection spreads behind the tonsils into the neck and chest. Swollen tissue can block the airway.) He died in May 1605. His death was a disappointment to all. He is credited with having done considerable work in the preliminary phase of the translation.

Robert Spaulding (Replaced Edward Lively as director of 1st Cambridge group after Lively's death)

Robert Spaulding was born in 1569. He graduated from Cambridge and was a rector in Edberton, Sussex. He was a junior dean at Cambridge until the death of Edward Lively, after which he replaced Lively as Regius Professor of Hebrew, appointed by King James I. Spaulding also followed in the footsteps of Lively by being appointed the director of the Cambridge group when Lively died in 1605.

John Richards

John Richards was born in 1564. He left home at fourteen years of age to attend Emmanuel College in Cambridge, from which he obtained a Doctor of Divinity in 1597. He was associated with the university and its colleges for his entire life. He was the rector of Upwell, Norfolk. King James, I appointed him as Regius Professor of Divinity. He was noted as a most excellent linguist.

He often participated in debates in the Latin tongue held in the great halls of the universities at Cambridge. He proved quite a scholar to all challengers.

Lawrence Chaderton

Lawrence Chaderton was born in 1537. He was born into a wealthy family who was staunch Catholics. He was destined to be a lawyer, so he moved to London, where he spent several years studying and practicing law. While in London, he became a protestant and forsook the law practice to enter Christ's College, Cambridge. He appealed to his father for financial aid, but his father sent him a bag with a coin and told him this was to be used to go a-begging. His father disinherited him of a large estate due to his forsaking the Church of Rome.

He was thoroughly skilled in Latin, Greek, and Hebrew and spoke Italian, French, and Spanish. He diligently studied the writings of the Rabbis as far as they aided him in understanding the Scriptures. He was at Hampton Court by invitation of King James. He was one of the four representatives of the Puritans.

Sir Walter Mildway approached Lawrence to help establish a new college in Cambridge. He agreed. Emanuel College came into existence in 1584, with Chaderton as the Headmaster. One of the students during his tenure was John Harvard, who would migrate to America and start Harvard University.

He died in 1640 at 103 years of age.

Frances Dillingham

Frances Dillingham was born in 1568. He enrolled at Cambridge when he was fifteen years of age. He became a dean at Christ College, where he was a lecturer in Hebrew. He was known as an outstanding Greek and Hebrew Scholar. He wrote for a publication for over twenty years and often wrote in defense of the Puritan point of view. He also published a manual on the Christian faith.

One of Dillingham's books was, *The Golden Key – Opening the Lock to Eternal Happiness.* In this book, he discusses marriage and how to make a success of it. He gives much advice to married men. The irony is that he was never married.

Roger Andrews

Roger Andrews was the brother of Lancelot Andrews. He went to Pembroke College in Cambridge nearly twenty years after his brother. He established himself as one of the brightest scholars and became the college's treasurer.

He was headmaster of Jesus College in Cambridge and served in that capacity for fourteen years. He was a famous linguist of the times. He received several opportunities to serve in various churches and on various boards. Even though Roger was twenty years younger than his brother Lancelot, it was an honor to serve as a translator on one of the greatest literary endeavors in history with his brother. The Andrews were the only siblings to serve together on the translation.

Thomas Harrison

Thomas Harrison was born in 1555. He became a student at Trinity College in Cambridge at 18 years of age. He would later become the Vice Headmaster of the same college. He was the Vicar of St. Andrews Church.

When writing about Harrison, McClure cited Dalechampio as follows: "On account of his exquisite skill in the Hebrew and Greek idioms, he was one of the chief examiners in the university of those who sought to be public professors of these languages."

Andrew Bing

Andrew Bing was born in 1574. He proceeded Geoffry King as Regius Professor of Hebrew for King James. Before this appointment, King James had recommended him for a position. He stated, "I am well aware of his worth." And he knew "it would be an honor and ornament to the university to choose him."

Bing was one of the youngest translators but extremely qualified. He was a professor of Hebrew at Trinity. He served as a rector at several churches.

THE THIRD COMPANY

The third company of translators was **Oxford group one.** They were assigned from Isaiah to the end of the Old Testament. There were eight men on this committee. John Harding was the director of this group.

John Harding (Director of the 1st Oxford committee)

John Harding was born in 1562. He started attending Magdalen College, Oxford, at the age of fourteen. He was the Regius Professor of Hebrew at Oxford and Rector of Great Hasley Church, Oxfordshire. He became president of his alma mater, Magdalen College.

The books this group was to translate were considered the most labor intense and problematic. Since men in this group were the most notable translators of the project, it was quite an honor and spoke of Harding's great ability to be named the director of this group.

John Reynolds

John Reynolds was born in 1549. He began attending Merton College at the tender age of thirteen and, by seventeen, was receiving a fixed amount of revenue from the college so that he might be devoted to special studies. Six years later, he was the Greek Lecturer in the college. Merton was founded in 1260 and claimed to be the oldest college in Oxford. This institution was strongly Catholic and resisted Protestant teachings.

Reynolds was a devoted Catholic for the early part of his life and sought zealously to convert his brother William from Protestantism to Catholicism. His brother, William, however, was just as diligent in his efforts to convert John to Protestantism. McClure said both were successful, "As a result of long conference and disputation, William became a Papist and so lived and died. While John became a Protestant and continued until his death to be a vigorous champion of the Reformation."

After his conversion, Reynolds was admitted into Corpus Christi College, where in 1580, he received his Doctor of Divinity. He would often debate Papist in public debates and was said to have soundly defeated several of their champions. He served as President of Corpus Christi College.

He was one of the four Puritans allowed by King James to attend Hampton Court and is credited as the father of the King James Bible, for it was Reynolds that suggested that the King mandate a new translation. Since this was not on the agenda nor looked on favorably by the bishops that were gathered together at Hampton Court, this was a bold move. He "moved His Majesty that there be a new translation of the Bible because those that were allowed in the reign of Henry VIII and Edward VI were corrupt and not answerable to the truth of the original."

This group met three days a week in John Reynolds's apartment, located over the arch entry to Corpus Christi College. This was undoubtedly due to his failing health, but he still attributed immensely to the translation. This they did until nearly the day of his death. He died in 1607 before the completion of the King James Bible.

Thomas Holland

Thomas Holland was born in 1539. He graduated from Oxford with a Doctor of Divinity and was Chaplin at Balliol College. He was appointed the personal Chaplin of Robert Dudley, who was given the position of Governor in the Netherlands.

Holland was appointed Regius Professor of Theology by Queen Elizabeth I. As a skilled debater in theology, he often held public debates at the College. These were, on occasion, attended by Queen Elizabeth I and later by King James.

Having proceeded through the classical education offered at Oxford, Holland became known as one "mighty in Scripture" and one so acquainted with the early church Fathers that it seemed as if he was one himself. Anthony Wood, a biographer of many notables of his time, said of Thomas Holland that some sip at learning while others drink of it, but with Holland, he was drowned in learning.

Richard Kilby

Richard Kilby was born between 1560-1561. He started attending Lincoln College, Oxford, when he was sixteen. In 1590 he was chosen as Rector of his college and remained in this position until he died in 1620. The position carried with it pastoral responsibilities, which were coupled with increasing academic endeavors. He was recognized as being so expert in Hebrew that in 1610 upon the death of his fellow translator, John Harding, he was appointed the King's Professor of Hebrew. He was also considered by Izaak Walton, a biographer, "a perfect Grecian."

He published a Latin Commentary on Exodus, chiefly drawn from the writings of the Rabbinical interpreters.

Miles Smith

Miles Smith was born in 1554. He was a student at Corpus Christi College. He transferred to Brasenose College and there obtained a Doctor of Divinity. He was a Chaplin at Christ Church and served as the Rector at various churches around Oxford.

Miles Smith was known as "a walking library." He was called by his contemporaries "an incomparable theologist." He studied all the writings of the Latin and Greek church fathers, over 300 manuscripts, and commented on them all in Hebrew. He was as well versed in Arabic, Chaldee, and Syriac as in English. It was said of Smith that he "had Hebrew at his fingers' ends."

He was chosen by the other translators to write the preface to the King James Bible, *Notes from The Translators to the Reader*. Concerning his fellow translators, he wrote: "There were many chosen who were greater in other men's eyes than their own, and who sought the truth rather than their own praise." Miles Smith, along with Thomas Bilson, served as one of the final editors of the King James Bible, perusing the entire text of the Bible before it went to press in 1611.

In 1612, King James I, appointed him Bishop of Gloucester. He died much lamented.

Richard Brett

Richard Brett was born in 1567. He attended Hart Hall in Oxford. When he was fifteen years old, he received his first degree. He then attended Lincoln College, where he continued until he received his Doctor of Divinity.

He was well-versed in Latin, Greek, Chaldaic (Aramaic), Arabic, and Ethiopian. He was the author of translations from Greek into Latin and wrote Latin tracts on church doctrine. Anthony Wood said of Brett, "He was a most vigilant pastor, a diligent preacher of God's Word, a liberal benefactor to the poor, faithful friend, and a good neighbor.

Mr. Fairclough (Daniel Featley), (Richard Fairclough)

Mr. Fairclough is a much-debated character by biographical researchers. While the earliest list of translators refers to Mr. Fairclough, Anthony Wood and some later writers, such as McClure, conclude this Fairclough was not Richard, but Daniel Featley, also known as Daniel Fairclough. According to McClure, this was distinctly asserted by his nephew, Dr. John Featley. Who authored a book entitled Dr. Daniel Featley Revived.

The main point of controversy is Mr. Fairclough's age. If this were indeed the translator, he would have been only 22 years old at the beginning of the translation. This is considerably less than the age of most of his associates. He was also quite a proficient author, but he never mentioned working on the translation in his writings.

The second option is that Richard Fairclough was the translator. He would have been about 52 or 53 at the time of the translation. He was an unknown but very capable linguist. He also lived in Oxford at the correct time.

Both were qualified, both were pastors, both held a Doctor of Divinity, and both were fluent in English, Hebrew, Latin, and Greek.

William Thorne (brought in after 1604)

William Thorne was born in 1569. He graduated from New College in Oxford and was a rector or vicar of seven different churches. He was the Dean of Chichester Cathedral for 29 years and was a published author and poet.

Thorne succeeded John Harding as Regius Professor of Hebrew at Oxford. For his doctoral disputation in 1602, Thorne defended the position of the Church of England on the canonicity of the Bible, not knowing he would soon be one of the translators. Thorne was also one of the King's Chaplains.

Anthony Wood, a biographer, stated that Thorne was "reputed not only for his incomparable skill in oriental tongues but also for other learnings." Besides being an expert in Latin, Greek, and Hebrew, he was also versant in Syriac, Arabic, and other languages.

THE FOURTH COMPANY

The fourth company was **Oxford group two**. They were assigned the four Gospels, Acts, and Revelations. There were eleven men in this group. The director of the group was Thomas Ravis.

Thomas Ravis (Director of the 2nd Oxford committee)

Thomas Ravis was born in 1560 and graduated from Christ Church College in Oxford. He was vice chancellor at Oxford for two terms and appointed Dean of his college, Christ Church. He held many prestigious positions, but perhaps none as rewarding as the Bishop of London.

He was the director of the second Oxford group, demonstrating the translators' respect and confidence in him. He died before the translation was complete.

George Abbot

George Abbot was born in 1562. He entered college at fourteen, graduated from Balliol College, Oxford, and was later dean.

He was a lecturer, author, and poet. He delivered a series of lectures on the book of Jonah at the University Church, which lasted five years. He published a Latin book and other works and was a bestselling author of the day.

He was installed as dean of Winchester and Vice Chancellor of the University. He was an excellent preacher but never pastored a church. He would become Bishop of London after Thomas Ravis died and was eventually named by King James the Archbishop of Canterbury, the highest position obtainable in the Church of England, the leader of the Church of England.

He attended Hampton Court Conference and, with much enthusiasm, endorsed Reynold's suggestion of a new translation.

Richard Eedes

Richard Eedes was born in 1554 and attended Christ's Church College, Oxford. He was a rector and was honored to be a Chaplain for Queen Elizabeth and King James. Queen Elizabeth said of Eedes, "he is the doctor for my soul."

Eedes attended Hampton Court Conference and was named as a translator but died in 1604 before the preparatory work began on the translation. He was the first translator to die.

John Aglionby (filled the vacancy of Richard Eedes after 1604)

John Aglionby was born in 1566. He graduated from Queen's College, Oxford. He was commissioned to fill the vacancy of Richard Eedes. He was a highly skilled debater and was said to be somewhat entertaining during the process. He was Headmaster at Westminster School and part of the committee that elected bishops and managed the business affairs of the Westminster Cathedral.

According to one biographer, "He was esteemed as one of the greatest of the Greek language of any that lived in that age and kept correspondence with learned men in every part of the Christian World."

He died in 1610 before the translation was published. The translation was in the final stages of review and editing. He was a major contributor to the work.

Giles Tomson

Giles Tomson was born in 1553 and graduated from University College, Oxford. Giles held many prestigious positions in his lifetime. He was one of Queen Elizabeth's chaplains and frequently preached in her presence. Two impressive positions he held were his appointment as Dean of Windsor and his appointment as the Bishop of Gloucester.

He attended Hampton Court Conference and was in favor of the new translation. He was said to have taken many pains in translating the four Gospels. He was under heavy responsibilities during this time and passed away in 1612, only a few months after the publishing of the King James Bible.

Leonard Hutten (brought in after 1604)

Leonard Hutten was born in 1557 and graduated from Christ Church College, Oxford. He was a rector at three different churches, the last of which was in Northamptonshire. He held this post for over 30 years until his death.

Hutten was a scholar of substance, being described as "an excellent Grecian." His knowledge of Greek stood him in good stead in his role as translator.

James Montagu (brought in after 1604)

James Montagu was born in 1568 and graduated from Christ's College, Cambridge. He became Headmaster of Sidney Sussex College. He also became the personal chaplain of King James and was Dean of the King's Chapel. It has been said that no clergyman had more influence on King James than Montagu.

Montague attends the Hampton Court Conference as the Dean of the Royal Chapel. He was unquestionably a sound scholar.

Henry Savile

Henry Savile was born in 1549. He enrolled in Brasenose College in Oxford at only twelve years of age and then later transferred to Merton College, Oxford, to finish his education. He was excellent in science, Greek, English, early church history, and theology.

He translated early scientific and mathematical manuscripts and historical and religious material. He published an eight-volume edition of the writings of the early Church Fathers of Chrysostom. His translation of Roman history was a bestseller.

Savile was the only translator that was not a clergyman. He was, however, a devoted Christian and a Greek scholar.

He became known as Sir Henry Savile as King James knighted him.

John Peryn

John Peryn was born around 1558 and graduated from Saint John's College, Oxford. He was appointed Regius Professor of Greek at the University while serving as a Greek reader at his college. He maintained the Regius Professorship until his death.

He was a vicar of at least two churches.

Ralph Ravens

Ralph Ravens was born in about 1557 and graduated from Saint John's College, Oxford. While little is known of this translator, he was a vicar of three different churches and was grounded in Latin, Hebrew, and Greek.

John Harmar

John Harmar was born in 1555 and graduated from New College, Oxford. He was Regius Professor of Greek at Oxford. He published an English translation of Beza's sermons. He often took part in debates with Catholic Theologians in Paris. In 1586 Harmar was responsible for the first Greek book printed at Oxford. It consisted of several sermons from John Chrysostom. He became the Headmaster of his alma mater.

Not only was Harmar involved in the translation, but he was chosen as one of the men who would be a final reviewer of the complete translation.

THE FIFTH COMPANY

The fifth company was **Westminster group two**. They were assigned the Epistles of the New Testament. There were eleven men in this group. The director was William Barlow.

William Barlow (Director of the 2nd Westminster committee)

William Barlow was the director of Westminster group two. He graduated from St. John's College in

Cambridge and then transferred to Trinity Hall College to receive his B.D. and D.D. He served as a scholar, teacher, and administrator while at Trinity.

Among his many honorable accomplishments, he was appointed to a chaplaincy by Queen Elizabeth, appointed the Bishop of Rochester, and made Dean of Chester College. He also published several books and pamphlets.

Barlow attended the Hampton Court Conference and was the official chronicler of the conference. His summary of the event was titled, *The Sum and Substance of the Conference* and was published in May of 1604. McClure stated that Barlow was actively employed in the preliminary arrangements of the King James Bible. And by taking part in the work, he brought "a thoroughbred scholar to the work."

John Spencer

John Spencer was born in 1559 and graduated from Corpus Christi College, Oxford. He was appointed Greek Reader at the College and served as secretary to the President of the College. He was also a vicar at various churches in Oxford and was appointed by King James as one of his Chaplains. Spencer was elected as President of Corpus Christi College after the death of John Reynolds, a fellow translator.

Spencer was said to attend very carefully to the literary execution of the translation. So much so that the translation began to engross his attention. He left off all other duties so that he might focus only on the King James Bible translation.

Roger Fenton

Roger Fenton was born in 1565 and graduated from Pembroke College, Cambridge. He was a rector at various churches in his lifetime, including one pastorate near his hometown of Lancashire.

Fenton preached before King James on at least three occasions. These sermons were published after his death. He published several works, including A Perfume Against Noisome Pestilence, during the plague.

One biographer of Roger Fenton noted that as a theologian, "he placed primacy on the Holy Ghost in Christianity, and in each person coming to an understanding of the Spirit's work." Fenton believed that the faithful Christian must search diligently to find specks of sin and be continually active in repentance."

Ralph Hutchinson

Ralph Hutchinson was born in 1552 and graduated from St. John's College, Oxford. He was elected president of his alma mater and served for sixteen years until his death.

Hutchinson died in 1606 just as the translation was getting underway. His contributions are not known, if any.

William Dakins

William Dakins was born in 1569 and graduated from Trinity College, Cambridge. He was a vicar and was appointed a Greek lecturer at Trinity College. He was an expert in ancient languages.

Dakins, who would have been an immense aid in the translation, died in 1607.

Michael Rabbet

Michael Rabbet was born in 1552. He was rector at St. Leonard Parish Church in Steatham, Surrey, and continued in this service for 46 years. He was named a University preacher at Cambridge.

Thomas Sanderson

Thomas Sanderson was born in 1561 and graduated from Magdalen College, Oxford. He then transferred to Balliol College, Oxford, to finish his education. He was the vicar of St Lawrence Jewry Church, located in London.

In 1601, Thomas's brother John obtained an old Pentateuch manuscript from a Jewish Priest. On returning to England, he presented it to his brother.

Nicolas Felton (brought in after 1604)

Nicolas Felton was born in 1563 and graduated from Pembroke Hall, Cambridge. He was eventually appointed Headmaster of Pembroke. He was the rector of several churches and chaplain under Queen Elizabeth and King James.

Felton had a high aptitude for the Greek language and, at 23, was appointed Greek Lecturer at his college.

Arthur Lake (brought in after 1604)

Arthur Lake was born in 1567 and graduated from New College, Oxford. He was the pastor of several parishes and was eventually the Bishop of Bath and Wells. He was elected as vice chancellor of New College.

A biographer noted that he was "well read in the Fathers" and "had such a command of the scriptures that few went beyond him in his time."

After his death, several of his sermons were published.

Nicolas Love (brought in after 1604)

Nicolas Love was born in 1568 and graduated from New College, Oxford. He became the Headmaster at Winchester College in 1601.

Love was vicar of various churches and was appointed as a chaplain to King James.

Although Love was not listed as an original translator, he is mentioned on various occasions as taking part in the translation. Upon final review of the manuscripts, Miles Smith expressed his intent to have Love closer at hand during this final editing.

He was known as a Greek Scholar.

George Ryves (brought in after 1604)

George Ryves was born in 1559 and graduated from New College, Oxford. He was named Warden of the college and Vice-Chancellor. He was a rector of various churches.

Ryves gave an impressive sermon oration at Oxford in Latin, which King James attended. The King, who spoke Latin fluently, was so impressed that he compelled him to be a chaplain to the King, where he could hear him more frequently.

He is thought to be a later addition to the translators to fill a vacancy.

THE SIXTH COMPANY

The sixth company was **Cambridge group two.** They were assigned the Apocrypha. There were seven people in this group. The director of the group was John Duport.

While this company translated the Apocrypha, viewed as a non-inspired work, they also reviewed the translations of every other group. So, they had a definite influence on the work as a whole.

John Duport (Director of 2nd Cambridge committee)

John Duport was born in 1550 and graduated from Jesus College, Cambridge. He was the director of the second Cambridge Group.

Duport began his studies at Jesus College and remained there his entire life. He went from being a student to being Headmaster of the school and held many posts in between. He also served as Vice-Chancellor.

He held a position as pastor at several churches and presided over the disciplinary committee at the university. He devoted himself tirelessly to the church and university.

William Brainthwaite

William Brainthwaite was born in 1563 and graduated from Emmanuel College, Cambridge. He taught at the university for several years. Brainthwaite would eventually become Headmaster of Gonville College and Caius College. His highest honor was being elected Vice chancellor at Cambridge University.

Brainthwaite was renowned as a scholar with unique expertise in Greek. His library consisted of over fourteen hundred volumes, still intact at the various colleges he administered.

Jerimiah Radcliffe

Jerimiah Radcliffe was born in 1552 and graduated from Trinity College, Cambridge. He not only received a Doctor of Divinity from Cambridge, but he also received one from Oxford. He was appointed Vise Master of Trinity College.

He pastored three churches simultaneously, which was not uncommon during this era.

Samuel Ward

Samuel Ward was born in 1572 and graduated from Emmanuel College, Cambridge. In 1611 he was named Headmaster of Sidney Sussex College, Cambridge. Sussex University was the most Puritan-leaning university in Cambridge.

Ward was appointed as Royal Chaplain to King James. He also served as a rector at various churches. A biographer's assessment of Ward was that "he was clear in judgment and of great skill in the languages, especially Hebrew."

He kept a diary, and due to this fact, much is known of Samuel Ward's personality, motivations, and views. Many of his writings, letters, and sermons have been preserved.

Andrew Downes

Andrew Downes was born in 1553 and graduated from St. John's College, Cambridge. He was appointed Regius Professor of Greek at the University and served in this capacity for thirty-nine years.

His comrades referred to him as the ablest Grecian of Christendom.

John Bois

John Bois read entirely through the Hebrew Bible by age five and, by age six, was writing Hebrew legibly and in fair character. He was often found studying Greek at the Cambridge library from four a.m. until 8 p.m. (sixteen hours a day). Bois tutored many of his fellow students at the University in Greek. His classes were also attended by many of his Greek professors.

John Bois served as pastor of St. John's Church before, during, and after his work as a Bible translator. He preached without notes but not without much prayer and study. He had the entire Greek New

Testament committed to memory. He practiced fasting twice a week and often gave to help the poor until he had no more to give himself. Among Bois' writings was a commentary in Latin on the Gospels and Acts.

Even after his retirement, he spent eight hours every day studying and mostly reading and correcting ancient authors. He took notes of all the proceedings during the translation. His notes are some of the only evidence we have today, telling us how they went about things. He left at his death as many leaves of handwritten manuscripts as days he had lived, over 30,000 pages of writings.

John (Robert) Ward

John Ward was born in 1569 and graduated from King's College, Cambridge. He taught at the school and was a part of the administration. He was a rector of various churches. He was also a close associate with fellow translator Lancelot Andrews.

Closing Words from the Translators

The following are the closing comments of, *The Translators Note to the Readers*:

> "Gentle reader, we commend thee to God, and to the Spirit of His grace. He removeth the scales from our eyes, the veil from our hearts, opening our wits that we may understand His Word, enlarging our hearts, yea correcting our affections, that we may love it above gold and silver, yea that we may love it to the end. Ye are

brought unto fountains of living water which ye digged not. Others have labored, and you may enter into their labors; O receive not so great things in vain, O despise not so great salvation! It is a fearful thing to fall into the hands of the living God; but a blessed thing it is and will bring us to everlasting blessedness in the end, when God speaketh unto us, to hearken; when He setteth His Word before us, to read it; when He stretcheth out His hand and calleth, to answer, Here am I, here we are to do thy will O God."

CHAPTER 10

THE METHOD OF TRANSLATION

We have expounded on the rules used by the scribes while copying the Old Testament Scriptures to ensure their accuracy. Now we will examine the method used by the translators of the King James Bible to ensure the New Testament was an accurate rendering of the originals in English.

A new English Bible was being considered because there was such a variance in the publication of the Bibles. To clear up the differences and to publish a Bible that would be consistent with the originals. King James issued a resolution at the Hampton Court Conference which read, "That a translation be made of the whole Bible, as constant as can be to the original Hebrew and Greek; and this to be set out and printed, without marginal notes, and to be used in all churches of England in time of divine service." *1

The resolution stated, "as constant as possible to the original Hebrew and Greek." The translators used what is called verbal equivalence. This means the words in Hebrew and Greek were rendered as close as possible to English, both in form and definition. This is also called a word-for-word translation. This allows the reader to interpret the Scriptures for themselves. Nothing is added to nor taken away from God's Word.

Modern versions of the Bible use a method called dynamic equivalence. This means translating not word for word but thought for thought. A word or phrase that is equivalent based on the translator's interpretation. This leaves room for errors. They often change the form of a word, bringing a noun over and changing it to a verb. They insert a word they feel should be added or take away entire portions of scripture that they view as needless. By paraphrasing the Word of God, they have not simply updated the language but have diluted the content, often to such an extent that the foundational doctrines of the Bible are called into question.

After the Hampton Court Conference, the translators spent the next three years doing preliminary preparation. This included gathering original manuscripts, research, contacting and securing the help of other learned men and pastors, and most importantly, prayer and fasting. In 1607 the translators were divided into six groups; two met at Cambridge, two at Westminster, and two at Oxford. Each of the six groups was assigned a Bible portion that their group was to translate.

Under the direction of King James, Richard Bancroft, Archbishop of Canterbury, set forth fifteen general rules for the guidance of the translators. These rules were to ensure the integrity of the translation.

RULES TO BE OBSERVED IN THE TRANSLATION OF THE BIBLE *2

1. The ordinary Bible read in the church, commonly called the Bishops' Bible, is to be followed and as little altered as the truth of the original will permit.

The first rule called for the Bishop's Bible, the official Bible of the Church of England, to be followed and only altered in the text where the translation was not in agreeance with the original Hebrew or Greek.

2. The names of the prophets, and the holy writers, with the other names in the text, are to be retained as nigh as may be, accordingly, as they are vulgarly used.

The second rule was to ensure that the names in the Bible remained the same. That the pronunciation of a name and the identification of an individual would not be affected by the translation. The word vulgarly, as it is used here, means "as it is generally used, applied, or accepted."

3. The old ecclesiastical words to be kept, the word church not to be translated as congregation.

Rule three was important, especially during this time in history. The translators were all of Protestant, Puritan, or Anglican faith, and they often changed the word church to congregation. This was justified in many of their eyes because, in that era, if anyone wrote of the Church, it was often a reference to the Catholic Church. This rule ensured that the original, old ecclesiastical words were translated correctly, despite the current misinterpretation of any word.

4. When any word hath divers significations, that to be kept which hath been most commonly used by the most of the ancient fathers, being agreeable to the propriety of the place, and the analogy of faith.

Rule four dealt with words with various meanings. As in English, Hebrew and Greek words often had several definitions. When determining the correct definition, the translators were instructed to keep the meaning commonly inferred by the ancient church fathers and to use context clues. The word also must be in agreeance, and not contradictory, with other scripture.

5. The division of the chapters is to be altered either not at all or as little as may be if necessity so required.

Rule five stated that the Bible was not to be altered as far as the number of chapters in a book and the number of verses in a chapter. It also protected the Bible from realigning chapters in a different order.

6. No marginal notes at all to be affixed, but only for the explanation of the Hebrew or Greek words, which cannot, without some circumlocution, so briefly and fitly be expressed in the text.

Rule six addressed one of the main points of contention surrounding the Geneva Bible. These marginal notes were slanted heavily toward Calvinism. No marginal notes were allowed but only the explanation of the Hebrew or Greek words, which could not be expressed in the text.

7. Such quotations of places to be marginally set down as shall serve for the reference of one Scripture to another.

Rule seven allowed for scripture references to be added in the margin of the Bible. These references were to refer the reader from one scripture to another that was similar or referred to the same event.

8. Every particular man of each company to take the same chapter or chapters, and having translated or amended them severally by himself, where he thinketh good, all to meet together, confer what they have done, and agree for their part what shall stand.

Rule eight stated that each translator had to independently translate the books assigned to his group. Each man had to translate every book, every chapter, every verse himself. This displays the qualifications of these men. Though there were scholars who excelled in certain languages beyond their peers, they all had to be proficient enough in Hebrew and Greek to complete this task on their own.

Next, the entire group would review the books together. Every verse would be examined, and the translations would be compared. They would critique the translation until there was a consensus that they had the correct wording.

9. As any one company hath dispatched any one book in this manner, they shall send it to the rest to be considered seriously and judiciously; for his majesty is careful in this point.

Rule nine, after the group completed their translation and review, a copy of the approved translation would be sent to the other five groups for their evaluation. Once the translated book was given to one of the other five groups, the entire group would go over the text together.

It was stated in this rule that King James was careful about this point. King James felt that to maintain the integrity of the Bible. Every group must review; this would keep any group from being influenced within their group to accept an inferior translation of any text.

10. If any company, upon the review of the book so sent, doubt or differ upon any place, to send them word thereof, note the place, and withal send their reasons; to which if they consent not, the difference to be compounded at the general meeting, which is to be of the chief persons of each company, at the end of the work.

Rule ten says that after every other company had reviewed the book, it was returned to the original group with notations of any place of doubt or difference. The place was to be duly marked, and reasons given for their differences. All differences still in question would be determined at the general meeting of chief persons. This group consisted of two leaders from each of the six groups, and they solved any remaining problems.

11. When any place of special obscurity is doubted of, letters to be directed by the authority to send to any learned man in the land for his judgment in such a place.

The eleventh rule allowed letters to be sent to any learned man in the land for their judgment concerning any obscure or ancient word whose meaning was in doubt. This included but was not limited to Hebrew and Greek professors, accomplished linguists, and renowned scholars of the day.

12. Letters to be sent from every Bishop to the rest of his clergy, admonishing them of this translation in hand; and to move and charge as many as being skillful in the tongues; have taken pains in that kind, to send his particular observations to the company, either at Westminster, Cambridge, or Oxford.

Rule twelve encouraged letters to be sent to every bishop and clergy admonishing those skilled in linguistics to send any observations to the group that was translating those Scriptures into which they had an insight.

13. The directors in each company, to be the Deans of Westminster and Chester; for that place, and the king's professors in the Hebrew and Greek in either university.

Rule thirteen gave direction as to the assignment of the directors of each company. They were to be the Deans of Westminster and Chester Universities and the King's professors of Hebrew and Greek. In the biographical sketches of the translators, you will read of several translators that were Regius Professors of Hebrew or Greek. This means they were appointed by King James to that position and were supported financially by the crown. These appointments were extremely limited and very prestigious.

14. These translations are to be used when they agree better with the text than the Bishops' Bible: Tyndale's, Matthew's, Coverdale's, Whitechurch's [Great], Geneva.

Rule fourteen allowed the translators to use other previously published Bibles for references, such as Tyndale's New Testament, Coverdale's Bible, The Great Bible, and the Geneva Bible.

15. Besides the said directions before mentioned, three or four of the most ancient and grave divines in either of the universities, not employed in translating, to be assigned by the vice-chancellor, upon conference with the rest of the heads, to be overseers of the translations, as well Hebrew as Greek, for the better observation of the 4th rule above specified.

Rule fifteen was added to help ensure adherence to rule number four. It allowed for three or four of the most respected and sober theologians, who were not employed in the translation, to be assigned, overseers. This was just another step to ensure the integrity of the Bible.

Richard Bancroft, who had been appointed as overseer of the project by King James, would be responsible for the final review and for delivering the Bible to the printer. However, Bancroft died in 1610. It is probable that Bancroft could not finish the review before the bible was delivered to the printer. Since

Bancroft could not finish the review, a committee of two was appointed; they would be responsible for the final review to check for punctuation, spelling, and general appearance. This committee was made up of Myles Smith and Thomas Bilson. Bilson was thought to have replaced Bancroft as neither one was listed as one of the translators.

<u>In conclusion, every verse of the Bible was carefully examined and decided upon fourteen times.</u> This made it impossible for translators to impose their viewpoints on a passage. A translator had to have a valid reason to persuade every other scholar before a change would be accepted. There was no private interpretation allowed. (2 Peter 1:20-21)

CHAPTER 11

THE 1611 EDITION

Contents

The King James Bible, when completed, consisted of a Title Page, a Dedicatory of the Bible to the King, Notes from the Translators to the Readers, various tables and calendars, The Old Testament, the Apocrypha, and the New Testament.

The title page of the original 1611 King James Bible was very elaborate.

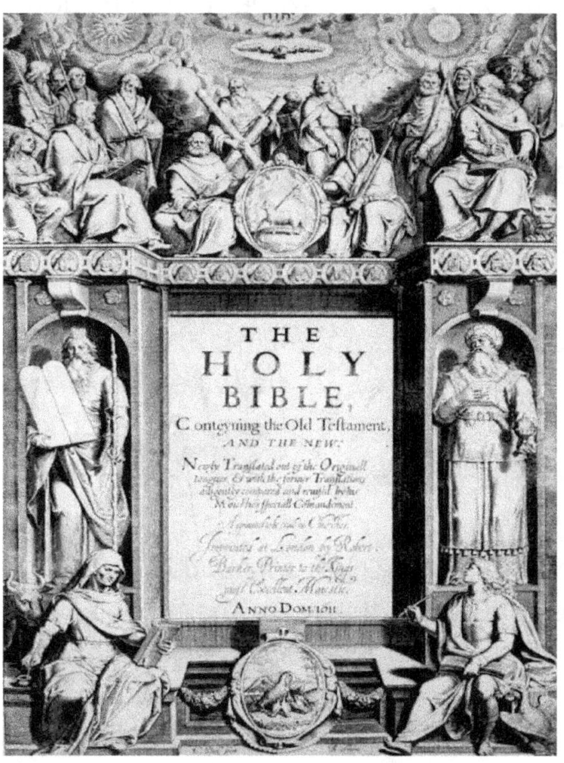

The imposing architectural frame, suggestive of a church edifice, is full of human figures, including Moses and Aaron, the Evangelists, and the Apostles. Traditionally, Jesus had twelve Apostles, but the thirteen depicted here include Matthias, who replaced Judas after his betrayal (Acts 1:26), and Paul, who described himself as an Apostle in Romans 1. Each apostle is represented by a symbolic attribute, though not all are easily identifiable.

The Dedicatory was a letter to King James, giving him honor and thanks for not letting the resolution of Queen Elizabeth for a new English translation of the Bible go unfulfilled. It stated that King James had shown great religious affection but none more forcible than the vehement desire to accomplish and publish this work. The last paragraph reads, "The Lord of heaven and earth bless your majesty with many and happy days, that as His heavenly hand hath enriched your Highness with many singular and extraordinary graces; so, you may be the wonder of the world in this later age, for happiness and true felicity, to the honor of the Great God, and the good of his Church, through Jesus Christ, our Lord and only Saviour."

Next were the Notes from the Translators to the Readers. Miles Smith wrote them. This eleven-page preface was a defense of the necessity of a new English translation. Smith wrote. "Translation it is that openeth the window, to let in the light; that breaketh the shell, that we may eat the kernel; that putteth aside the curtain, that we may look into the most Holy place; that removeth the cover of the well, that we may come by the water, even as Jacob rolled away the stone from the mouth of the well, by which means the flocks of Laban were watered."

There were also various calendars and tables. One table consisted of a twelve-month guide to use when reading the Bible. It suggested which passages should be read in the morning and which in the evening. It had a table you could use to determine what day Easter would fall in any given year. And a couple of charts of the scriptures to be read on certain Holy Days.

The Old Testament was next. It was the translation of the original Hebrew canonized books. There were 39 books in all.

Between the Old and New Testaments was the Apocrypha. It was translated from Greek and Latin and was inserted for historical purposes only. These books were not canonized. They were later removed for three main reasons. First, they were often mistaken as inspired scriptures because they were included in the Bible. Many people assumed that they were God's Word. Secondly, they were contradictory to the Bible. And third, no copy of the Hebrew Scriptures ever contained them or referenced them.

The Catholic Church proclaimed these books as inspired and still included them in their Bible. Many practices and doctrines of the Catholic Church are based on the Apocrypha: prayers for the dead, the immaculate conception, the doctrine of purgatory, and salvation by penitence. The origin of these books is unknown, but they mysteriously appeared around 80 AD.

And finally, there was the New Testament. It was translated from the original Greek canonized books. There were 27 books in the New Testament.

Italicized Words

You will also notice italicized words throughout the King James Bible. Those who would like to question the authenticity of the King James Bible would point out that these were words that the translators added to the original text. This is true. But let us examine the reasoning behind the insertion of these words.

These italicized words are not normally written in Hebrew but were inserted in conversation. Words that every Hebrew knew to insert to make a thought complete. Since the translators did not want to add or take away from the text, these words were italicized to alert the reader of their insertion. To show the necessity of these words in conversation, notice that when Jesus quoted the Old Testament from the original Hebrew, He was quoting from a text that did not have the italicized words. However, his quotation inserted the words italicized in the King James Bible. In English, we must have these words inserted to complete the thought.

Examples:

Matt. 4:4, "But he answered and said, It is written, Man shall not live by bread alone, but by every **word** that proceedeth out of the mouth of God." In **Deut. 8:3**, we see the phrase he quoted, "but every *word* that proceedeth." Notice **word** is italicized in the Old Testament, but not in the New Testament. So, **word** was not in the Hebrew written text, but when Christ spoke, he knew to insert it in conversation.

John 10:34, "Jesus answered them, Is it not written in your law, I said ye **are** gods?" In **Psalms 82:6**, the phrase reads, "Ye *are* gods." Notice again, *are*, is italicized in the Old Testament, but not in the New Testament. So, Jesus would have read from Hebrew, *"Ye gods."* But Jesus inserted the word, are, in his conversation to complete the thought.

2 Sam. 21:19, "And there was again a battle in Gob with the Philistines, where Elhanan the son of Jaareoregim, a Bethlehemite, slew *the brother of* Goliath the Gittite, the staff of whose spear was like a weaver's beam." The words, the brother of, are italicized. If these words were omitted, the Bible would say that Elhanan slew Goliath instead of Goliath's brother, which would be contradictory to the fact that David slew Goliath. In **I Chron. 20:5**, you can verify that it was indeed Goliath's brother, Lahmi, by name, that Elhanan slew. Sadly, *The New World Translation* of the Bible leaves out these italicized words, causing no end of confusion to its readers.

Without the insertion of these words, the translators would have taken away from the Scriptures. These words are understood and excepted as a necessary part of translation. Even modern translators know these words should be in the Bible and do not question their placement.

To further explain the italicized words, I will use my late aunt Francis as an example. Aunt Francis was born deaf. When communicating with her through sign language, she would not sign certain words, but if you were to tell someone what she was signing, you would insert those words. Instead of signing, "I need to go to the store with you," she might sign, "I go to store you." You would understand the unspoken words, and when speaking to someone else about her request, you would insert the unspoken words to complete the thought.

So, the italicized words were not simply words that the translators added in an attempt to change the text, but instead, they were inserted to clarify the text for English-speaking people.

Printing

Upon completion, the Bible was taken to the King's Printer, Robert Barker, in 1610. Barker had inherited this position from his father, Christopher Barker, who was the printer for her Majesty Queen Elizabeth I.

This was a very lucrative business. A printer would purchase a manuscript, and then all the proceeds from selling the books would go to the printer. Barker is said to have paid £3,500 for the King James Bible. King James funded all the translating process expenses, such as salaries, materials, and travel expenses.

Work certainly proceeded very quickly, as the first edition is dated 1611. Barker used five printing presses to accomplish this amazing publishing feat.

The first two printings were large folio Bibles for use in churches. They were exceptionally large: approximately 17" tall and 30" wide when opened, and they weighed up to 30 pounds, but smaller editions were soon produced for personal use, starting in 1612.

The original printing sold for 10 shillings loose-leaf or 12 shillings bound. The printing was substandard, with uneven lines, and the black letter typeface was considered inferior. It also contained many mistakes, as the proofreading of the text was not as thorough as it should have been.

He Bible

The very first printing became known as the 'He Bible.' It rendered the Scripture in Ruth 3:15 as, "he went into the city," instead of, She went into the city.

Wicked Bible or the Adulterous Bible

The worst mistake of all occurred in 1631. The word, not, was omitted from the seventh commandment so that it read, Thou shalt commit adultery. The whole imprint was recalled, and Barker was fined £300. This Bible became known as the Wicked Bible or the Adulterous Bible.

It seems that the project was jointly funded with Bonham Norton. Because in 1618, a series of lawsuits ensued between Barker and Norton and their varying business partners. Norton seems to have held shares in the royal printing business, and trouble broke out over the shares. Books and bibles printed between 1617 and 1629 carried a bewildering series of printers' names; sometimes Barker with a partner, sometimes Norton with the same partner – or a different one! It was difficult to tell who the King's Printer was until Robert Barker was confirmed in the office in 1629. However, Norton accused Barker of taking a bribe. Barker was found guilty of the accusation, fined, and imprisoned, dying in prison in 1635. *1

The Acceptance of the King James Bible

The King James Bible, or the Authorized Version as often called, was meant to replace the Bishops' Bible as the official version for readings in the Church of England. It was 'appointed to be read in churches.' The King's printer issued no further editions of the Bishops' Bible, so King James supplanted it as the standard Bible for church use in England.

The Bible's acceptance by the general public took a little while. The Geneva Bible continued to be popular. There was a final printing in England of the Geneva Bible in 1616. Still, large numbers were also imported from Amsterdam, where printing continued up to 1644. The Geneva Bible contained notes from the translators in the margins of the Bible. Since the King

James did not have marginal notes, It became known to the people of England as the Bible without notes.

As the acceptance of the King James Bible accelerated, it began affecting day-to-day conversations. People began to adopt phrases that have gained a place in everyday English today. Such phrases as; 'my brother's keeper;' 'how are the mighty fallen;' 'out of the mouth of babes;' 'the skin of your teeth;' 'fly in the ointment;' 'no peace for the wicked;' 'physician heal thyself;' an 'eye for an eye,' and 'the blind leading the blind' –all of these are in the King James Bible. Also, the influence that the King James Bible exerted on the English language can be deduced from the fact that it occupies nearly 42 pages of the *Oxford Dictionary of Quotations*.

Over one billion copies of the King James Bible have been sold since 1611. It is the number one bestseller of all time.

CHAPTER 12

EDITIONS SINCE 1611

Six Editions

The King James Bible has had six editions. Critics often ask, which King James Bible do you use, 1611, 1629, or perhaps 1769? This attempts to prove that the King James Bible has been revised. However, **The King James Bible has never been revised. It has been edited, which is a significant difference.**

The First Edition

The first edition was published in 1611 by Robert Barker. There were several printings of this edition by various printers in England and abroad. Because of the crudeness of the printing process in that era and the printers' carelessness, many words were misspelled, and punctuation was altered. Printing was a slow and complicated process. All type was set by hand, one piece at a time (one piece at a time through the Bible), and errors were an expected part of any completed book.

The Second Edition

The second edition was published in 1629. It was the first ever printed at Cambridge. It was edited by two original translators, John Bois and Samuel Ward. The purpose of this second edition was to correct the spelling and printing errors. There was not any revision of the text.

The Third Edition

The third edition, like the second, was also at Cambridge and was published in 1638. It served the same purpose as the second edition, to correct printing errors, and was stage two of the 1629 edition. These two editions were only seven years apart.

The Fourth and Fifth Editions

The fourth and fifth editions were published in 1762 and 1769 at Cambridge. These editions updated spelling and grammar but did not revise the text.

The Sixth Edition

The sixth edition was published in 1873 in Cambridge. Dr. F. H. A. Scrivener meticulously standardized the 1769 edition from 1866 to 1873. Resulting in the Bible, we use today. So, if asked, you use the 1873 Cambridge edition of the 1611 King James Bible.

The King James Bible Has Never Been Revised

I stated earlier that the King James Bible has never been revised but has been edited. This is an especially crucial point. People trying to defend various bible revisions often mention that the King James Bible has been revised over 1000 times. This is not true. It has been edited but never revised. Let me explain the difference.

When a book is revised, it means it is changed from the original. When the author of a book revises his work, he is trying to correct an error or add information that was left out. Since God empowered these holy men of old to write the books of the Bible, as the Holy Ghost moved on them, there is no error or incompleteness in the Bible. When the translators, which used copies of the original Scripture, translated the Bible, they did not revise the words but put them into English with the exact same meaning as they had in either Hebrew or Greek. When the King James Bible was published, there was never an attempt to alter the meaning or form of a word. A verb was kept a verb, and a noun was kept a noun.

When a book is edited, it is corrected in spelling, punctuation, capitalization, and grammar. It is to correct the proofreading and printing process's flaws but not change the book's content.

A few examples of spelling correction in our 1873 Cambridge edition versus the 1611 first edition would be as follows.

The old English spelling of 'pass' was 'paffe,' so 'it came to pass' in the 1611 edition would read, 'it came to paffe'. By correcting the spelling to a standardized spelling, the Bible is edited but not revised.

Love is spelled loue in the 1611 edition.

Ever is spelled euer in the 1611 edition.

Jesus is spelled Iefus in the 1611 edition.

Joy is spelled ioy in the 1611 edition.

These are just a few words edited to a standardized spelling in 1873. As you can see, these were changes in the editing process, but no revision was made to the text.

Almost all examples of spelling corrections were made in the second edition. One example was in Psalms 69:32, 'Seek good' was changed to 'seek God.' When the editors looked back at the original manuscripts, they quickly realized the printer had made two errors; he had capitalized seek instead of 'God' and had misspelled 'God' as good. Both corrections were made, but the text was not revised. It was edited to match the original.

The wayes side was edited to read the way side. This was, again, a printer error that was corrected.

Ecclesiastes 1:5, 'the place' was a printing error in 1611 and was corrected to 'his place.'

An example of punctuation editing can be demonstrated by a phrase found in the 1611 Translation. The phrase read, *which was of our father's,* this was changed to *which was our fathers.* The apostrophe should not have been in the text, but it was a printing error. As you can see, these were necessary edits to keep the King James Bible accurate to the original.

Famous Printing Errors

Some of the famous printing errors that have appeared in the various printings of the King James Bible obtained a nickname.The Wicked Bible (1631) omitted "not" in "Thou shalt not commit adultery" in Exodus 20:14. The Printer's Bible (1702) read "printers have persecuted me" instead of "princes" in Psalm 119:161 The Vinegar Bible (1717) read "The Parable of the Vinegar" instead of Vineyard. The Ears to Ear Bible (1810) read, "who hath ears to ear let him hear" in Matt. 14:43. The Rebekah's Camel's Bible (1823) read, "And Rebekah arose, and her camels [should be damsels]" in Gen. 24:61. *1

The New King James Bible is not another edition of the King James Bible. It is a revised Bible. It was published in 1979 by Thomas Nelson Publishers. It ignores the Textus Receptus over 1200 times. There are 22 omissions of the word 'hell,' 23 omissions of the word 'blood,' and 44 omissions of the word 'repent.' The terms: devil, damnation, and JEHOVAH are entirely omitted. It is estimated that the New King James Bible makes over 100,000 translation changes or about three changes per verse. There are footnotes giving credence to the Wescott and Hort Greek New Testament.

Parallel Bibles are popular today. These Bibles will print the King James Text next to another version of the Bible for comparison. These hold no merit, as they confuse the reader instead of clarifying. No one would place a rotten apple in a barrel with good apples. If you realize that the King James Bible is God's inspired Word, then no other versions of the Bible can complement it or improve upon it.

CHAPTER 13

REVISED VERSIONS

The question arises. If the King James Bible is God's original words in English, Why are there other versions of the Bible?

In 1611, there were only a handful of English Bibles in print, but because of the variance among them, there was a demand for one Bible; a Bible that everyone could use, a bible that would do away with confusion over Scriptures, a bible that could be trusted. Once the King James Bible was published, it became that bible. And for a couple of centuries, it had no rivals until 1881. Once the Revised Version was published, it opened up a floodgate of various versions. Now, instead of desiring everyone to have the same Bible, there are nearly 400 versions from which to choose. What has brought us to this place of confusion?

Brooke Foss Westcott and Fenton John Anthony Hort

One reason for revising the Bible is that someone disagrees with its message. When they find it contrary to their lifestyle, they want to change the word of God to fit their lifestyle instead of changing to fit God's word. Let us examine the lives of two men, Brooke Foss Westcott and Fenton John Anthony Hort, who published a Greek New Testament in 1881.

These two Anglicans held views that contradicted the fundamental ministers of the day. They disagreed with the Bible from Genesis through Revelation. Westcott denied the truth of Genesis chapters 1-3. He wrote to the Archbishop of Canterbury on March 4, 1890: 'No one now, I suppose, holds that the first three chapters of Genesis, for example, give a literal history. I could never understand how anyone reading them with open eyes could think they did' *1

Hort concurred with Charles Darwin's theory of evolution. He wrote on April 3, 1860, 'But the book which has most engaged me is Darwin. Whatever may be thought of it, it is a book that one is proud to be contemporary with ... My feelings is strong that the theory is unanswerable' *2 Hort denied a literal Eden. He wrote. 'I am inclined to think that no such state as Eden ever existed.' *3

This is only the beginning of Westcott's and Hort's disagreements with the King James Bible. Wescott stated, 'I reject the infallibility of Holy Scriptures overwhelmingly.' * 4 He said in 1847, 'I never read an account of a miracle, but I seem instinctive to feel its improbability and discover some want of evidence in the account of it.' Hort said, 'Mary Worship and Jesus Worship have much in common.' *5

These men held many views that complied with the Catholic Church's doctrine. Hort said, 'The pure Romanish view seems nearer and more likely to lead to the tru NIV th than Evangelical.' *6

These men also founded several occult societies, two of which, The Hermes Club and The Ghostly Guild, claim to communicate with the dead. *7

Since they opposed the Bible, they decided to write their own Greek New Testament. They used two manuscripts, the Vaticanus (discovered in the Pope's library in 1481) and the Sinaiticus (discovered in 1859 in the trash at St Catherine's monastery on Mt. Sinai), as their main sources. These two texts were Catholic manuscripts that contradicted each other over 3000 times in the gospels. *8

There have been many revisions of the bible, but I chose to mention these two men as my example of men who revised it to change its doctrine because every revised Bible since the Westcott and Hort Greek New Testament that has been published has used this Greek New Testament as their source for the New Testament, either completely or in part. DR. D. A. Waite's book, Heresies of Wescott and Hort, is a tremendous resource to view the deadly effect that Wescott and Hort had on the Bible.

One day while working as a chaplain at our local hospital, I was talking to a lady who was distressed about God's direction for her life. After hearing her predicament, I advised her to get a Bible and read certain passages.

She responded, "I've read the Bible, but it doesn't seem to help me."

So, I ask, "Did you read from a King James Bible?'

A look of fear came on her face, and she said, "Oh no! I cannot read from the King James Bible. Every time I do, it is like God is speaking to me."

I replied, "Isn't that what you need, for God to speak to you."

Do not try to find a version that lines up with your way of thinking and living, that makes you feel good about yourself, but rather read the King James Bible and let God's Word accomplish its purpose in your life.

Hebrews 4:12,

"For the word of God is quick, and powerful, and sharper than any twoedged sword, piercing even to the dividing asunder of soul and spirit, and of the joints and marrow, and is a discerner of the thoughts and intents of the heart."

Financial Gain

Another reason for revised Bibles is the financial gain that comes through their publication. Since the King James Bible is the best-selling book of all time, with over a billion copies, it makes sense that if someone can publish a bible and the public moderately receives it, it will profit millions of dollars.

NIV

The New International Version (NIV) exemplifies questionable motives for financial gain. The NIV was first published in 1978. It was marketed among Protestant denominations as a bible to reach the common man in common language. It quickly becomes a best seller. Over 400 million copies have been sold since 1978. They began to revise the Bible more dramatically and in several ways. In 1985 it was revised because their understanding of the manuscripts had changed. So, everyone had to buy a new bible and rememorize the scriptures that they had previously memorized. In 2011 another version came out, which was gender-neutral. And now, you must purchase the newest version, the 2022 NIV Bible, and relearn the Scripture you thought you had memorized.

Can you imagine the confusion if the children were given an assignment in Sunday school to memorize a portion of Hebrews 2:17. One child would stand up and quote from King James, "to be made like unto his brethren." Another would quote from the 1978 NIV, "to be made like his brothers." Another would stand and quote from the 2011 NIV, "to be made like his brothers and sisters." But at last, a student would settle the issue with his new 2022 NIV. He would quote, "to be made like them, fully human in every way."

The love of money has been the motivation behind most of the revised Bibles. The Word of God should not continually change to align with the current market. It would help if you questioned the motives of these publishers.

Another reason for the revised Bibles is notoriety. As we studied the beginnings of the translation of the Bible into English, we viewed men who were hated, persecuted, incarcerated, and even put to death to translate and publish the Bible. But in the last 150 years, it has become a badge of honor among colleagues to publish a Bible with your name attached to it as an editor.

The Jefferson Bible,

One such Bible was called, *The Life and Morals of Jesus of Nazareth* or *The Jefferson Bible*, by Thomas Jefferson. Jefferson was the third president of the United States of America. Along with John Adams, Benjamin Franklin, Robert Livingston, and Roger Sherman, he penned the Declaration of Independence. He is considered one of the most influential founding fathers of America.

In 1820, he created the Jefferson Bible. Jefferson considered himself a Christian but did not agree with many of traditional Christianity's views. While often portrayed as a highly religious man. His religion consisted of his own Bible that was custom-made by him. Jefferson viewed Jesus as strictly human, a great moral teacher, but not divine.

Taking a penknife, he pored over the biblical text in Greek, Latin, French, and English, and then specific passages were cut out from two volumes of Jacob Johnson's 1804 King James New Testament printing. He then pasted those passages together to create the Jefferson Bible. *9

He removed all references to miracles and eliminated the resurrection story from the bible. No mention of demon possession or supernatural events, such as healings, remained in the Scripture. It went from 27 books to an 84-page pamphlet.

So proud was he of this work that he wrote to John Adams that he had trimmed away "the corruptions of schismatizing followers" to arrive at "the most sublime and benevolent code of morals which has ever been offered to man" *10

Jefferson's Bible is not widely used today, but his cut-and-paste mentality remains strong. It is important to remember that the Bible was never intended to be a buffet to choose the most delectable parts; it was meant to be taken as a whole or not at all.

I close this chapter with the most often-heard reasons for a new and improved Bible among the laity. People will often complain that the King James Bible is archaic. That all the thee's and thou's are too hard to understand. While I do not belittle anyone who has trouble comprehending the King James Bible, I will tell you that the effort it takes to dig out the treasure is well worth your time and effort.

Someone once said, "God will give you a steak, but He won't cut it up and feed it to you."

Samuel Gipp said,

"God has gone to all the trouble to inspire the perfect originals. He has collated the books of the Old Testament and New Testament and documented their authenticity. He has preserved His words against attack from Roman Catholic tyrants and Alexandrian philosophers. This process has cost Him the lives, homes, and families of some of His most faithful servants. He assembled the best scholars in history and had them translate the Bible into the world's language (English) in its purest form." *11 Considering all

God has done to allow us to have a King James Bible in our possession, surely, we can take the time to search out its treasures.

With the King James Bible, the responsibility of interpreting the Bible falls on the reader. So, the Bible exhorts us in 2 Tim. 2:15,

"Study to shew thyself approved unto God, a workman that needeth not to be ashamed, rightly dividing the word of truth."

Whereas with the various revised bibles they have interpreted the Scripture for you, they have taken all of the work out; no need to pray or study about the meaning of a passage, no need for a dictionary or a concordance, no need to shew thyself approved, its already been done for you. If you do not have a King James Bible, let us hope they interpreted it correctly in the Bible you chose because your eternity depends on it.

The booklet titled Bible Word List, published by the Trinitarian Bible Society of London, England, lists 618 words, uncommon words from the King James Bible. There is a brief definition of each word. And a daily bible reading plan is included in this booklet. The booklet is handy to keep in your Bible. You can purchase one of these at tbsbibles.org for a minimal cost.

The five reasons a revised Bible should not be used in our daily Bible study or churches.

1. They cause widespread confusion.
2. They discourage memorization, for they are all different.
3. They provide an opportunity for perverting the truth. They are not all right with all the different slants on the Scriptures.
4. They make it challenging to teach the Bible. When everyone in your church is reading from a different bible, it is challenging to be unified in studying God's Word.
5. The most significant reason is that the King James Bible has never been proven incorrect.

The End

ENDNOTES

Chapter 1

*1- W. A. Waite, Defending the King James Bible, Th.D., PH.D. 2nd edition 1998 Pg. 6

*2 David Ewert, From Ancient Tablets To Modern Translations,1983 pg. 44

*3 Salomo A. Birnbaum, *The Hebrew Scripts Volume 2*, Palaeographia, 1954

*4 G I Davies, M. N. A. Bockmuehl, D. R. de Lacey, A. J. Poulter, *Ancient Hebrew Inscriptions, Corpus, and Concordance*

*5 Charles Butterworth, The Literary Lineage Of the King James Bible, 1941 pg. 4

*6 David Ewert, From Ancient Tablets To Modern Translations, 1983 Pg. 20

*7 *Wikipedia*, History of Paper

*8- David Ewert, From Ancient Tablets To Modern Translations,1983 Pg. 62-63

*9 H. S. Miller, *General Biblical Introduction*,1960, Pages 184-185

Chapter 2

*1 Christian Ministries International, *Is the Bible the Inspired Word of God*

*2 Lewis S. Chafer, *Systematic Theology*, I, pg. 68

*3 John F Walvoord, *The Holy Spirit*, Pg. 59-60.

Chapter 3

*1   David   Scudder,   *Smoking   the   Bible*, bethelchapelchurch.com, Aug. 29,2016

*2 Steve Rudd, Aramaic Chronicle of Theophanes the Confessor, Diocletian 19th year

*3 Lee Martin McDonald, James A. Sanders, Editors: *The Canon Debate*; Everett Ferguson, Factors Leading to the Selection and Closure of the New Testament Canon, p 317, 2002

*4 Lee Martin McDonald, James A. Sanders, Editors: *The Canon Debate*; Everett Ferguson, Factors Leading to the Selection and Closure of the New Testament Canon, p 318, 2002)

*5 D Lortsch, Historie de la Bible en France, 1910 pg. 14

*6 David W. Cloud, Rome, and the Bible: Tracing the History of the Roman Catholic Church and Its Persecution of the Bible and of Bible Believers, Way of life Literature, copyright 1996

*7 Alan Confino, *Why the Nazis Burned the Hebrew Bible*. Commentary, June 2014

*8 Kristallnacht, *Night of Broken Glass*, United States Holocaust Memorial Museum

*9 Ann Taylor, *World War II: Before The War*, The Atlantic. (19 June 2011)

*10 Perry Chiaramonte, Reporter for Fox News, March 15, 2016

*11 Voice of Martyrs, Bartlesville, Ok. www.persecution.com

*12 Catherine Hezser, Jewish Literacy in Roman Palestine

*13 Robert E, Sutton, AMIT magazine, Oct. 8th, 2015

*14 Timothy B. Lee, 40 Maps that Explain the Roman Empire, Aug. 19, 2014

*15 *Ancient Greece and Rome*: An Encyclopedia for students (4 volume set), page 257

*16 Tyler C Eskelson, *State, Institutions, and Literary Rates in Early Modern Europe,* Journal of Education and Learning, Vol.10 No. 2; 2021

Chapter 4

*1 Dr. Kenneth Barker, *How We Got the Bible*, Helpmewithbiblestudy.org, 2001

*2 H. S Miller, *General Biblical Introduction,* 1960, pg. 184-185

*3 Emilie Le Beau Lucchesi, *Discover*, Sep. 28, 2022

*4 Scrivener, Frederick Henry Ambrose *(1884). The Authorized Edition of the English Bible, 1611, its subsequent reprints, and modern representatives.* Cambridge: Cambridge University

*5 Norman Geisler, *Inerrancy,* 1978; *A General Introduction to the Bible*, 1986; and *From God to Us*, 2012.

*6 Samuel C. Gipp, Th. D., *Alexandria or Antioch*, All Message Series, Apr. 23, 2021

*7 Jack Moorman, Forever Settled

*8 Rev. W A Waite Th.D., Ph.D., *Defending the King James Bible*, June 1998, 6th Printing, Pg. 40

*9 H. N. Arkell, Providential Preservation of the Text of the New Testament, Hark Ministries, 2005

*10 W H Wyatt, A Study of the King James Bible, Pg. 2

*11 Samuel C. Gipp, Th. D., *Alexandria or Antioch*, All Message Series, Apr. 23, 2021

Chapter 5

*1 Dennis Leap, *How God Preserved the Bible*, Philadelphia Trumpet, Sept-Oct. 2005

*2 Ernest L Martin, *Restoring the Original Bible*, chapter 12, third edition, 1994, online version

*3 Fred R Coulter, Canonization of the Old Testament, A Faithful Version, 2022

*4 Canon of Scripture, *Unger's Bible Dictionary*, p. 178

*5 Ernest L Martin, *Restoring the Original Bible*, chapter 12, third edition, 1994, online version

*6 McDonald and Sanders, The Canon Debate: On the Origins and Formation of the

Bible, pp. 267-268

*7 Little, C.T., editors (1955). *The Oxford Universal Dictionary*. Oxford University Press. Williams. Onions

*8 Herman L Hoeh, Do We Have the Complete Bible,1974

*9 Jerome, Jerome's preface to the books of Solomon

*10 Ryan Leasure, Why the Apocrypha is not in the Bible, Cross examined, Sept 16. 2018.

*11 Alexander Wilson McClure, *The Translators Revived*, Pg. 185-186

*12 Bruce, F.F. *The Books and the Parchments: How We Got Our English Bible*, Old Tappan, NJ: Fleming H. Revell, 1950 pg. 164.

*13 Dr. Samuel Gipp, An Understandable History of the Bible

Chapter 6

*1 Baugh, Albert (1951). *A History of the English Language*. London: Routledge & Kegan Paul. pp. 60–83.

*2 Donald Brake, *A Visual History of the English Language*, Grand Rapids MI: Baker Books, 2008. Pg. 40

*3 Donald Brake, *A Visual History of the English Language*, Grand Rapids MI: Baker Books, 2008. Pg. 41

*4 Donald Brake, *A Visual History of the English Language*, Grand Rapids MI: Baker Books, 2008. Pg. 43

*5 Andrew Miller, *Miller's Church History*, Addison, IL: Bible Truth Publications, 1999, pg. 637

*6 Bruce Shelly, *Church History in Plain Language*, Dallas TX: Word Publishing, 1982 Pg. 225

*7 Donald, L. Broadbent, *The Pilgrim Church*, Grand Rapids, MI: Gospel Folio Press, 1931 pg. 138-140

*8 Timothy Paul Jones, *Christian History Made Easy*, Torrance, CA: Rose Publishing, 2009 Pg. 97

*9 English Bible History, GreatSite.com, an online showroom of the Bible Museum.

*10 Donald Brake, *A Visual History of the English Language*, Grand Rapids MI: Baker Books, 2008. Pg. 47,66

*11 Bryan Ross, www.gracelifebible-church.com, Wycliffe, July 18th, 2011

*12 Christianity Today, *Christian History*, John Hus, 2000, Issue 68

*13 David Roach, Baptist Press, Theology and Doctrine, Erasmus' Greek NT Changed History 500 Years Ago, March 8, 2016

*14 David Beale, Pictorial History of the English Bible, 1982, pg. 20

*15 Alexander Wilson McClure, *The Translators Revived*, Pg. 22-23

*16 Biblical Heritage Exhibit, *History of the English Bible*, Miles Coverdale, Jan. 1, 2017

*17 David Cloud, *Way of Life Literature*, P.O. Box 610368, Port Huron, MI 48061, Sep. 14, 2010.

Chapter 7

*1 King James I, Biography, Jesus-is-lord.com

*2 David, Matthew, *James the I. King of England and Scotland*, Encyclopedia Britannica.

*3 Cambridge Texts in the History of Political Thought King James VI and I Political Writings

*4 1604, *Workes* pp. 211-222

*5 1604, *Workes* pp. 81-89

*6 Stewart, 182, 300–301.

*7 Charles I of England, Wikipidia.com

*8 Robert Stedall, The Challenge of the Crown, 2012

*9 King James, *Basilicon Doron*

*10 1604, *Workes* pp. 340

*11 Samuel C. Gipp, *The Answer Book*, 1989

*12 Mark Cartwright, *James I of England*, World History Encyclopedia, April 28, 2021

*13 King James I, Biography, Jesus-is-lord.com

Chapter 8

*1 Hampton Court Conference, Wikipedia

*2 Millenary Petition, Editors Encyclopedia Britannica

*3 Dr. Laurence M Vance, *A Brief History of the King James Bible*, Vance Publications.

*4 *Gentleman's Magazine and Historical Chronicle* Volume XXXVIII for the Year MDCCLXVIII. (August 1768) By Sylvanus Urban, London, pp 373, who quotes the folio source.

Chapter 9

*1 Bill Bradley, *The Translators of the King James Bible*, Safegaurdyoursoul.com

*2 Alexander Wilson McClure, *The Translators Revived*, 1853

*3 kingjamesbibletranslators.org

*4 Gustavus, S Paine, *The Men Behind the KJV*, 1959

*5 Adam Nicolson, *God's Secretaries*, 2003

*6 William P Grady, *Final Authority*, 1993

Chapter 10

*1 Dr. Laurence M Vance, *A Brief History of the King James Bible*, Vance Publications.

*2 *Gentleman's Magazine and Historical Chronicle* Volume XXXVIII for the Year MDCCLXVIII. (August 1768) By Sylvanus Urban, London, pp 373, who quotes the folio source.

Chapter 11

*1 Wikipedia, Robert Barker, King's Printer

Chapter 12

*1 Way of Life Literature, *Changes to the KJV since 1611*, Aug 17, 2010.

Chapter 13

*1 David Fuller, *Which Bible*, 1st ed., pg. 191

*2 David Fuller, *Which Bible* 1st ed., pg. 189

*3 David Fuller, *Which Bible* 1st ed., pg. 191

*4 Wescott, The Life, and Letters of Brook Foss Westcott, Vol1, pg. 207

*5 Hort, Life and Letters Vol 2, pg. 49-51

*6 Hort, Life and Letters Vol 1 pg. 77

*7 James May, Wescott, Hermes, and Occult, 2005

*8 D A Waite, Heresies of Westcott and Hort, pg. 2

*9 Alyssa Roat, Christianity.com, *What is the Jefferson Bible?* Jul 10, 2019

*10 Letter to John Adams, October 12, 1813, National Archives.

*11 Samuel C Gipp, *The Answer Book*, 1999, 5th printing, pg. 103

ABOUT THE AUTHOR

Pastor Stephen R. Gentry has been active in ministry for over 35 years. He served as a full-time evangelist for eight years, preaching revivals, camp meetings, and conferences across the United States and abroad. He has nearly twenty-five years of pastoral experience. Pastor Gentry founded and served as administrator for Summit Christian Academy, a Christian school in Millbrook, Alabama. He currently serves as Pastor for Westside Holiness Church in Douglas, Georgia.

Pastor Gentry has accompanied and supported missionaries in Mexico, Costa Rica, and the Dominican Republic. Bro. Gentry serves as president of Harvest Season Ministries, Inc. President Gentry's dedication to HSM has led to tremendous growth in all areas of ministry in the Dominican Republic during his tenure.

Bro. Gentry has studied the translation of the King James Bible for many years and has taught in various churches on this subject and on the radio.

Bro. Gentry and his wife Rochelle have been happily married since 1990. Rochelle has been the perfect example of a godly wife. She has supported her husband with much love and prayer.

Contact information
(912) 381-9949
brostevegentry@hotmail.com.

Stephen R. Gentry
40 Baymeadows Drive
Douglas, GA 31535

www.ingramcontent.com/pod-product-compliance
Lightning Source LLC
Chambersburg PA
CBHW070800160726
48004CB00001B/263

9 798987 359310